Praise for *High-Velocity Digital Marketing*

"If you want to remain steeped in the traditional four Ps approach in marketing, this book isn't for you. However, if you are ready to step up and build a high-velocity digital marketing strategy that quickly produces results, read on."

—David Meerman Scott, entrepreneur, business growth strategist, and best-selling author of twelve books, including *Fanocracy* and *The New Rules of Marketing and PR*

"The best marketing business book of the year! Steven Kahan delivers. He inspires. *High-Velocity Digital Marketing* is a testament to Kahan's profound grasp of digital marketing. Marketing leaders will reap the benefits of this book for years to come."

—Kevin Klausmeyer, current or past Board Member of multiple companies including KnowBe4, Jamf, Cloudera, Callidus Software, Sourcefire, and Quest Software

"*High-Velocity Digital Marketing* is a compelling guidebook to accelerating revenue at reasonable cost. Marketing methods are changing fast, and Steven is at the forefront. He delivers valuable insider knowledge and shares today's best strategies to be wildly successful in modern sales and marketing."

—Mike Triplett, Managing Director of Insight Venture Partners

"Steven is an exceptional marketing innovator and practitioner. His high-velocity marketing strategies are methodical, comprehensive, and modern. Given today's fragmented and pervasive marketing landscape, Steven provides a clear process for developing the focus and creative energy required to execute successful marketing strategies and campaigns."

—Darren Guccione, CEO & Cofounder of Keeper Security

"Steven Kahan is an experienced and knowledgeable CMO who shows marketers how to connect with buyers and build crazy-effective digital marketing strategies. I've seen companies of all sizes follow Kahan's guidance and surpass their biggest and best-funded competitors. This marketing technology playbook will level the playing field."

—Jonathan Cogley, Founder of LogicBoost Labs

"Yet again, Kahan has written a how-to on accelerating revenue growth based on years of doing it at some of the most successful technology companies on the planet—a compelling read that provides practical, step-by-step strategies to market in ways that create authentic connections with B2B buyers throughout their purchase journeys. This book will profoundly change the face of today's business marketing."

—Josiah Sternfeld, CEO of Integrous Marketing

"By embracing the strategies in this incredible book, you will totally transform your business. I had a front row seat watching Steven Mark Kahan build a marketing strategy that drove massive sales—without a huge budget. Every company can benefit from reading this book."

—Hugh Burnham, CEO of Lumina Communications

"Kahan's command and control of the most winning go-to-market strategies through levering the optimal blend of technology, metrics, and management is unparalleled. The application of these principles is in large part directly correlated to the success I have enjoyed in selling for the past twenty years."

—Damon Tompkins, Chief Revenue Officer of Delinea

"Finally, a no-fluff marketing book written to help CMOs take the ideas presented and put them into action immediately. Kahan pairs a valuable and insightful look into today's buyer journey with a detailed playbook that shows marketers exactly how to win revenue against tough competition."

—Philip Vorobeychik, Managing Director of Vertica Capital Partners

"This is absolutely the best book on the new world of marketing. *High-Velocity Digital Marketing* offers groundbreaking strategies that will reinvent the way CMOs support sales success. As I read it, I literally underlined every sentence. I went through two highlighters before I finished."

—Simon Azzopardi, CEO of WeScale Global

HIGH-VELOCITY
DIGITAL
MARKETING

Also by Steven Mark Kahan

Be a Startup Superstar

Learn How to Accelerate Revenue Growth Now

During his 30+ year career, Steven Mark Kahan has developed a high velocity digital marketing blueprint that has helped 7 start-ups quickly grow revenue and achieve successful exits, generating $5 Billion in shareholder value.

Because you've purchased this book, Steven is giving you FREE access to one of his most popular Marketing Masterclasses where you'll learn how to:

- Focus on your target audience's "must-solve" problem
- Craft a killer value proposition that expresses the value of your differentiation
- Build and deliver content that contributes to revenue growth
- Turn content into campaigns that deliver more leads, pipeline and revenue

To watch the Free marketing masterclass go to:
www.stevenmarkkahan.com

HIGH-VELOCITY DIGITAL MARKETING

Silicon Valley Secrets to Create Breakthrough Revenue in Record Time

STEVEN MARK KAHAN

Matt Holt Books
An Imprint of BenBella Books, Inc.
Dallas, TX

High-Velocity Digital Marketing copyright © 2022 by Steven Mark Kahan

All rights reserved. No part of this book may be used or reproduced in any manner whatsoever without written permission of the publisher, except in the case of brief quotations embodied in critical articles or reviews.

Matt Holt is an imprint of BenBella Books, Inc.
10440 N. Central Expressway
Suite 800
Dallas, TX 75231
benbellabooks.com
Send feedback to feedback@benbellabooks.com

BenBella and *Matt Holt* are federally registered trademarks.

Printed in the United States of America
10 9 8 7 6 5 4 3 2 1

Library of Congress Control Number: 2022018180
ISBN 9781637742167 (hardcover)
ISBN 9781637742174 (electronic)

Copyediting by Ruth Strother
Proofreading by Isabelle Rubio and Madeline Grigg
Indexing by WordCo Indexing Services, Inc.
Text design and composition by PerfecType, Nashville, TN
Cover design by Paul McCarthy
Cover image © Shutterstock / atk work
Printed by Lake Book Manufacturing

Special discounts for bulk sales are available. Please contact bulkorders@benbellabooks.com.

I'd like to dedicate this book to my wife, Terry, who loves me unconditionally, provides encouragement, and gives me the freedom to succeed in life. I can't imagine life without you.

CONTENTS

Contents

FOREWORD

In March 2020, all the in-person speaking engagements I had booked for the rest of the year were canceled, postponed, or shifted to virtual due to COVID. I had been accustomed to delivering some thirty or forty in-person talks around the world each year for more than a decade, so this was a huge change for me. Like many business owners when faced with disruption, I had to figure out what was next for me. I decided to focus on delivering talks at virtual events.

My online research suggested that I had to purchase a lot of new gear to make my virtual business work. A simple webcam feed stuffed into a Zoom room simply doesn't deliver a good virtual event experience. That meant I needed to up my presentation technology in a big way.

While I knew I wanted to install a high-end professional recording studio in a commandeered spare bedroom in my home, I didn't know where to start. To complicate things, my speaking style is a bit unusual. I needed to create a studio built around my preference to stand rather than sit while giving presentations. It was also important for me to display my slides on a screen next to me. I hated that virtual event platforms defaulted to slides being displayed in a huge window while the speaker is contained in a tiny secondary window.

So what did I do next? Likely the same thing you and millions of others would do. I started researching my options on the web. I also reached out to my professional network on social media to get suggestions for my home recording studio.

After a few weeks of careful research on dozens of websites, I ended up spending nearly $30,000 on gear. My buying process was conducted far away from any salespeople. All my decisions were based totally on what I had learned during my online research.

I find it fascinating that even in this marketing reality, most companies are still doing business the old way. They act as if it's still the 1980s and they are the experts, forgetting that people like me make B2B purchasing decisions based on independent research. Many of these old-school companies still focus on less effective techniques like cold-calling salespeople, exhibiting on trade show floors, and advertising in magazines.

No amount of investment in advertising, public relations, or salespeople could have influenced my recording studio purchase decisions. When I visited a website that was optimized just for making a sale, I quickly clicked away.

It's not just companies that are missing the modern marketing revolution. Universities are also reluctant to change, continuing to teach the old rules of marketing in their undergraduate and graduate programs.

Several years ago, I presented the ideas in my bestselling book *The New Rules of Marketing & PR* to graduate-level marketing students at a well-known university. After my talk, a woman approached me and asked if she could have a word in private. We went into the hallway, and she proceeded to break down in tears. She was so upset that she was unable to speak for a few moments.

When she gathered herself, she told me that nobody in her graduate marketing program had taught her about the modern marketing ideas I had shared with her class. Her marketing education had centered on the four Ps of off-line marketing: product, price, place, and promotion. She learned about television advertising, shelf space, and hiring expensive public relations firms. She was upset, she explained, because she felt she had lost tens of thousands of dollars in tuition and a year of her life to an educational program that was focused on outdated techniques.

We're in a new marketing world. Fortunately for marketers, executives, and students, Steven Mark Kahan's methods in *High-Velocity Digital Marketing* are centered on how to grow a business using the strategies and tactics that work to engage buyers like me when I was ready to spend a lot of money on a home recording studio. The core idea behind high-velocity digital marketing is simple: the quicker you convert leads into paying customers, the more successful your business will be.

In *High-Velocity Digital Marketing*, you will learn just how those companies that educated and informed me about what I needed to create a great home recording studio got me to spend tens of thousands of dollars in a few days. Instead of using interruption and coercion to make sales, Steve teaches methods for creating breakthrough revenue. He shares ideas that he has implemented to great success in his own and others' businesses. For example, Steve joined Thycotic as CMO when it was a new company that had closed only one six-figure deal. By implementing the ideas that you will read in these pages, Steve built programs that soon delivered several six-figure deals each quarter, and the team had even started to close seven-figure deals on a regular basis. All this success led Thycotic to eventually be acquired for $1.4 billion in 2021.

You can achieve similar success.

If you want to remain steeped in the traditional four Ps approach in marketing, this book isn't for you. However, if you are ready to step up and build a high-velocity digital marketing strategy that quickly produces results, read on!

David Meerman Scott

Entrepreneur, business growth strategist, and bestselling author of twelve books, including *Fanocracy* and *The New Rules of Marketing and PR*

www.DavidMeermanScott.com

@DMScott

INTRODUCTION

Marketers face a crisis. In a recent McKinsey survey, 83 percent of global CEOs said they expect marketing to drive most or all of a company's growth. Yet according to the *Harvard Business Review*, 80 percent of CEOs are dissatisfied with their marketing results, and CMOs have the highest turnover rate in the C-suite. In comparison, just 10 percent of the same CEOs feel that way about their CFOs and CIOs. Many sales and marketing leaders I've spoken with feel overwhelmed by revenue contribution expectations they cannot meet. These issues impact companies of all sizes from start-ups to the Fortune 50. Obviously, something is broken.

According to a survey by the Fournaise Group, CEOs know what the problem is but not how to solve it. Corporate leaders complained that their marketers often hole up in brand or social media bubbles instead of prioritizing vital business metrics like marketing's direct contribution to revenue growth. Of the CEOs polled, 70 percent acknowledged that they also were responsible for the lack of marketing performance, but they didn't know what to do to improve results.

While some underperforming marketers do continue to limit their focus to increasing engagement and "likes," that is not the whole story. In the beginning of the twenty-first century, three seismic shifts occurred, all inextricably tied to technology, that changed everything about marketing.

Yet few marketers understand these shifts, so they rely on outdated techniques and strategies that keep marketers sequestered in their bubbles. Many ultimately fail.

Don't despair. As much as these shifts have caused a crisis, they also present a huge opportunity. If you understand the shifts and how to market in the digital world, you will deliver more revenue growth at a lower cost. *High-Velocity Digital Marketing* reveals how to do just that, and in a more straightforward manner than you might expect. We start with the three seismic shifts, which are knowledge parity, digital dominance, and metric availability.

Knowledge Parity: The Leveling of the Playing Field Between Buyer and Seller

Until the early aughts, there was a wide knowledge gap between buyers and sellers. Sellers knew everything about their product and lots about their competitors. Buyers knew very little. At best, they knew somebody who used the product or came across an article in a trade magazine. For the most part, buyers relied on their gut and what the seller told them to make decisions.

The best marketers exploited this imbalance. They focused on finding creative ways to play to buyers' emotions to drive sales, while only highlighting the best parts of their products or services. This was the age of catchy slogans, taglines, and inspirational, funny, and cool campaigns—the age of Don Draper and *Mad Men*.

The ubiquity of the internet changed all that. Now buyers can access almost all the knowledge in the world in an instant. And, perhaps more importantly, they can read reviews. They can find thousands of unfiltered assessments from real customers and use them to inform their decisions.

In the B2B world, marketers can't hide aspects of their products or rely on emotional messages to persuade customers to purchase them. Of today's

B2B buyers, 67 percent no longer prefer to interact with a sales representative as their primary source of information. Instead, they gather information online through digital content. This means that to be successful, modern marketers must focus on creating thorough, transparent content that quickly connects with buyers and gets them to act. While this requires a pivot in strategy and tactics, it gives modern marketers like you a real chance to set the tone for the entire sales process. Take it.

Digital Dominance: The Centrality of Technology

Digital is the core of everything in marketing. It has gone from one of the things marketing does to *the* thing that marketing does. A Forrester research survey found that 62 percent of B2B buyers say they develop selection criteria for finalizing a vendor list based *solely* on digital content.

This shift is, in many ways, great news, but only if you understand how to exploit it. Digital technology makes it possible to reach much larger audiences and target them with far more precision than traditional media does. You can do this by leveraging marketing technology (Martech for short). But the Martech market has boomed, and it's difficult to know what technologies you must have. Even if you get the right ones, those technologies also can be difficult to master, which means that today's marketing leaders need to understand (and make sure their teams understand) how to use Martech to maximize return on investment.

Metric Availability: The Rise of Data and Measurement

The twenty-first century brought the birth of the data economy. Several of the most successful companies, including Amazon, Facebook, and Google, achieved their heights by selling, managing, and leveraging data. Few fields have felt the impact of data more than marketing. Marketers now can use the huge amount of personal information that exists on the web to create incredibly personalized and far more effective campaigns than ever before. And they can track the performance of specific ad buys and campaigns with an unprecedented degree of detail.

As such, many of the companies I've talked to (from small start-ups to the biggest Fortune 500 companies) claimed to be all about the data and metrics. Most have invested large sums in data-processing technologies, and some even have whole teams dedicated to statistical analyses and reporting. Yet, somehow, many struggle to find the answers to the most basic questions required to run effective marketing programs, such as:

- Where did my leads come from?
- How much did I pay (in either time or money) to generate those leads?
- How much revenue did those leads produce?

You would be shocked to know how many of the world's biggest companies can't answer these simple questions. According to HubSpot, only about 50 percent of marketers measure customer acquisition costs. To me, this is inconceivable. As a marketing leader, if you can't demonstrate return on investment, someone higher than you will reduce your budget, which ultimately shrinks marketing's impact and revenue growth. It becomes a vicious cycle. This book will help you get out of that cycle or ensure that you never enter it in the first place.

If you can master marketing data and measurement, you will score a huge advantage over your competition. Running marketing with poor measurement is like trying to solve a jigsaw puzzle in the dark. You grope for whatever piece you can find, and guess how it fits with everything else. A good measurement system turns on the lights. In this book, I will give you the switch.

Taken together, these three seismic shifts enable any business, no matter the size, to compete with the Goliaths of industry. While large companies could drown out competitors with massive TV, radio, and print ad buys in the past, smaller companies can now use marketing technology and highly targeted digital campaigns to quickly break through the noise and win big.

Over the course of my thirty years of experience running marketing for a few great technology companies, I have developed a unique marketing methodology that I call high-velocity digital marketing (HVDM). I got my first job as a CMO at the age of twenty-eight. At that point, digital marketing didn't really exist. As I progressed in my career, new technological capabilities popped up and developed. In many ways, the internet and I are contemporaries. We grew and developed together. I realized early on that my company could gain huge advantages from being among the first to master these new capabilities. But my teams and I had to figure it all out ourselves.

In the early 2000s, we experimented and cycled through hundreds of different campaigns and tactics. This book contains the outcomes of all that experimentation, refined strategies, and techniques I used to power rapid growth at company after company. It contains my distilled wisdom, so you don't need to go through the time-consuming, money-wasting trial-and-error period.

The concept behind HVDM is profoundly simple: the quicker you convert leads into customers, the more successful your business. Time is money, and velocity is the metric that reveals the most about both. Higher velocity means you're bringing in more revenue in less time. The higher the velocity, the faster your business can grow to greater heights.

A business that successfully implements a HVDM model runs like a well-oiled machine. It's a revenue-generating engine, and it requires constant tuning, testing, and tweaking to produce incredible results. That is exactly what we accomplished at cybersecurity software provider Thycotic, the last company where I served as CMO. Right before I joined, the company received an infusion of venture capital, despite that revenue had flat-lined for a couple of quarters. A quick triage of the situation revealed that Thycotic, like many other companies, had been relying too much on the old model of marketing and had done little to grow its digital presence. It spent a huge amount of money to acquire each customer, and its sales cycle was so pokey that it could never grow sales volume at the pace the new investors expected.

I also got lucky—Thycotic happened to have an exceptional marketing team in place. Everyone I inherited was creative, talented, and hard-working. They just didn't understand digital marketing. I retained almost every employee and brought in a few experts and longtime collaborators. We trained the team in HVDM and restored revenue growth the very next quarter. Thycotic went on to exceed our revenue targets every quarter for almost six years and grew nearly three times faster than the market. We even took market share away from brutally tough competitors, beating them in the biggest accounts where we had never competed before. We reduced customer acquisition costs and boosted deal velocity by more than 50 percent. We helped a lot of salespeople get pretty rich, and in a few years, we became rich ourselves when Thycotic sold for $1.4 billion.

This book is based on Silicon Valley insider marketing methods and provides the blueprint for modern B2B marketing in a fast-moving digital-centric world. It will show you how to build a digital marketing foundation and set in motion a modern marketing strategy to dramatically increase revenue growth for your company, no matter the size of your business or your industry. Businesses that adopt these practical strategies can unlock 25 to 75 percent of additional growth and trim 10 to 30 percent of their marketing costs.

I recommend reading this book from cover to cover so that you understand the interconnected nature of successful digital marketing. Chances are that it will inspire exciting new ideas for campaigns, strategies, approaches, and ways to position your company and products. Keep a notebook handy and record those ideas. Then assess your company and the way you currently market. Where are there gaps and weaknesses? Where can you improve and add velocity? What ideas can you leverage to produce quick wins? Work through the book, following the steps and the tips provided, and let everything feed your imagination.

Of course, the digital landscape changes constantly. But this book will give you a foundation in digital marketing best practices and show you how to recognize the seismic shifts as they evolve so you can ride the big waves they produce. It will show you how to face all the uncertainty with confidence. It provides several innovative, implementable methods to get found online and get buyers to purchase—fast. Every chapter is designed to unleash your creativity and excitement, to help you innovate, and to turn your company into a revenue rocket ship. I can only hope that this book helps you grow financially, professionally, and personally. That's what this journey is all about. And you deserve nothing less.

PART I

Build a High-Velocity Digital Marketing Foundation

CHAPTER 1

Laser Focus on Your Target Audience

Anytime a buyer goes online, they're inundated with ads and content such as pop-ups, videos, video ads, newsletters, emails, and product launch announcements. It is dizzying, numbing. A HVDM approach breaks through this cacophony to connect with buyers. The first step to making that connection is to understand exactly who the target audience is and what they need to get them to take action. Research shows that firms with a strong understanding of their audiences and competition are more than twice as likely to be high-growth businesses (those that grow at least 20 percent year over year). There are three keys to understanding your target audience: nail a niche, know their must-solve problem, and create a killer value proposition.

Nail a Niche

Everyone talks about finding their niche, but many companies fail to understand just how much it matters. Often, the companies that find and target a narrow, underserved segment of customers experience the most success. To start finding your niche, ask yourself who are your very best, most profitable current customers? Why do they buy from you instead of from competitors? Look for common characteristics, interests, and problems. This will indicate how your offerings deliver unique value to an ideal niche of buyers.

These were the questions we asked at Postini, an anti-spam software start-up I worked for. For readers too young to remember, in the early days of the internet, spam email was a massive problem. It wreaked havoc on the productivity of just about every worker who relied on email. It got so bad that local TV stations ran endless news spots about the spam pandemic. In response, several anti-spam companies cropped up, and Postini was one of them.

Almost every company needed anti-spam software. While we did sell to all sorts of businesses, I knew that for us to grow fast, we had to find an industry we could dominate. One of the most common spam messages advertised incredible new rates on mortgages. Most of the anti-spam software started blocking all emails that had something to do with mortgages. For most companies, this was great. But for banks, small lenders, mortgage brokers, and people in the process of buying or selling homes, it could be disaster. If a spam filter blocked those likely legitimate messages, banks might lose customers, and people might not close on their new house.

We happened to have a unique feature that allowed businesses to set the spam capture rate for specific words and phrases. In other words, a bank could decide to let emails about mortgages through. We realized that the thousands of small to midsize banks and mortgage brokers would be an ideal target audience for this unique capability, and we focused on marketing to them. This pivot inspired some fear in the sales team. They thought that we were closing ourselves off to potential customers since we'd already been closing deals across several industries.

We ultimately decided to specifically focus on banks and brokers. We learned how to speak their language. Buyers in our niche soon recognized us as leaders who better understood their needs, and they would talk about us to their peers. Sales rapidly accelerated. Soon it was almost impossible for our competitors to get a foothold in this segment of the market. Focusing on less helped us sell more. Once we established ourselves in that initial niche, we looked to branch out. We used a similar focused approach to go after different industries that had similar problems. Our highly focused strategy paid off, and eventually Google paid $750 million dollars to acquire Postini, and it used our software as Gmail's spam filter.

Finding a niche like the one above often requires a company to focus in on small segments of the market. Unfortunately, most companies avoid doing that because they fear that focusing on a smaller customer segment will limit their growth. I get it. It can be scary to focus and go all in on a smaller target audience. But if you try to be all things to all people, or even to a broad segment of people, you'll dilute your message. Nailing a niche is freeing. It enables you to develop a product road map with a go-to-market strategy, messaging, and content that will connect with ideal buyers instead of wasting money chasing people who probably won't buy anyway.

Of course, your niche can always grow. While I worked for Thycotic, we initially targeted the IT security and IT administration departments at mid-market companies in highly regulated industries. We chose highly regulated industries because the regulations require them to place a premium on IT security. We chose mid-market companies because we knew our bigger competitors didn't serve them. We could have tried to sell to larger companies early on. We might have even gotten ourseves into active sales cycles with a number of big businesses. While being considered for large contracts would have been exciting, we likely would not have won. At the time we were a young company that seemed like a risky bet. As we grew, we targeted and won deals with larger companies. So it's important to keep in mind that a niche could be your starting point; it doesn't have to be your fate.

Know Their Must-Solve Problem

Organizations typically understand the problems their products solve. It's always clear to them. But rarely can they differentiate what problems their customers see as nice to solve vs. should solve vs. must solve for their business. In the B2B world, customers typically spend money on must-haves. Most likely every part of your product isn't a must-have. If it were, you wouldn't need marketing. You need to identify a customer's must-solve problems, then highlight the parts of your products that solve those problems.

To know a customer's must-solve problem, you need to speak with as many current and prospective customers as you can. At Thycotic, whenever we got a new customer who seemed unique due to such characteristics as size or geography, I as the CMO would interview them as soon as possible. Further, I built my own customer advisory board, a group of our customers who were willing to answer my questions and give feedback about their experiences. The customer advisory board required a significant time investment from the customers, but they reaped a benefit: someone in the C-suite had their interests in mind. Most customers committed a significant amount of money to our company, and they wanted to ensure that their investment yielded the best possible returns. They could contact me with problems that did not get resolved to their satisfaction and talk about how we could help them succeed at a higher level. Since the best businesses keep their customers happy, this helped us perform better as well.

There is an art to interviewing customers. Many companies ask pointed yes or no questions such as would their life be better if they could do X faster?

Companies design these questions to get the response they want, which typically confirms their assumptions and makes their current strategy look smart. This reveals almost nothing about what the customer actually thinks or wants. I always prefer to ask open-ended questions and really listen to the responses. This strategy unearths new nuggets of information that helps the company adapt its products and positioning to stay ahead of its competitors.

I also made sure to ask the right questions to differentiate a must-have from a should-have or nice-to-have. I didn't call up and say, "What's your must-solve problem?" I sought to understand the entire context of their world. I created a system to discover the must-solve problem, where I would interview them about the following five items: status quo, problem, ideal solution, benefit, and impact.

The status quo represents the current situation, how they conduct business now. This matters because you don't often lose business to a direct competitor; you lose it to the status quo. Even if a customer doesn't work with one of your direct competitors, they likely rely on alternative solutions that at least partially solve their challenges.

Here are some examples of status quo questions:

- Describe your current process for X. What works? What doesn't?
- (For new customers) What were your operations for X before you hired us?
- How does your team stay on top of X or don't get overwhelmed by Y?
- What are a few of the tools you currently use? What do you like about them? What do you not like?

Then get the customers to describe their problem in their own words. Marketers often try to tell a customer what problem they have—typically because it aligns with a product they sell. That never works.

Sample problem questions include the following:

- What problems do you face when trying to do X today? Tell me more.
- How long has this been a problem?
- What solutions have you tried to implement? Did they work?
- What obstacles have you encountered to solving this problem?

If you believe you can solve their problem, dig further into their pain and ask about their ideal solution. This will provide you with a better understanding of what's most important to them.

Here are some sample ideal solution questions:

- How important is it to you or your organization to solve this challenge?
- What would be an ideal solution to this problem? Why is that the best solution?
- In a perfect world, how quickly would you solve this issue?

After that, you can ask what benefits they will receive from having the problems solved. Will they save time? Money? What's the opportunity cost? Take all the relevant information gathered about their status quo, the problems they have, and what their ideal solution looks like, and use that to tailor questions about the benefits of having their problems solved.

Here are some sample benefit questions:

- What impacts does problem X have on your business?
- What happens if you do nothing to solve it?
- What would it mean for you, your team, and your business to solve this problem?

Finally, the rubber hits the road when you ask about the impact. Never assume that the benefits expressed by target customers equates to impact. An impact can be a business impact or a personal impact. Saving time (benefit) can mean more time with kids. Or it can mean more productivity, more time to strategize and come up with unique ways to grow the business. Or both. The impact might be massive. For example, if we haven't secured this part of our business, we are vulnerable to hackers. Or if we don't make sure we comply to certain regulations, our business might receive huge fines. You need to find out if the impact is meaningful. This, ultimately, is how you identify a must-solve problem.

Sample questions about impact include the following:

- What would you do, or do more of, if you had more time in your day?
- How important is it to you, your team, and your organization to be able to do more?

In addition to listening for the problems, pay close attention to the specific language that customers use. Consider keeping a master document populated with the phrases that prospects and customers employ to describe their situation and problems. Then in your content and ads, reflect that language. One of the major advertising fallacies is that a unique or unusual way to describe products stands out and wins more customers. The truth is that in the B2B world, buyers don't care how clever the marketing department is. They want to work with someone who understands them and empathizes with them. Speaking their language proves that you do that.

While talking to customers is the best way to understand them, it is hardly the only way. I considered it part of my job as a CMO to be on top of all the current trends in the industry. I read (or at least skimmed) the trade publications, listened to podcasts, watched videos and webinars, and went to conferences and trade shows. I also maintained close relationships with analysts who covered our industry. These analysts spend hours speaking with customers, compiling and analyzing reviews, and examining customer outcomes to write their reports. Few people know more about customer pain points. I wanted to know exactly what my customers were thinking about at all times. That level of preparation often paid off in a big way.

Wedge Problems

In your research into customer problems, you might discover an issue that comes up repeatedly. But it might not be a must-solve problem, or you might not offer a must-have solution. Don't ignore all the chatter you hear, because this hot-button issue might offer a unique opportunity. I call these wedge problems. They are often new challenges that nobody in the market has a solution to. Smaller companies can respond quickly, develop the first solution, and use these issues to wedge their way into a crowded marketplace.

For example, when I worked for PentaSafe, we were a relatively young and small cybersecurity start-up trying to establish ourselves in a crowded market. We offered a set of products similar to our larger competitors and knew that we would never win a feature or function war against them. They had much larger R&D departments and would always be able to out-develop us.

At the time, the news was full of stories detailing how human vulnerabilities (i.e., employee errors) directly led to many successful hacking attacks. Stories reminding people to update their passwords or with headlines like, "Passwords: A Necessary Evil" regularly appeared in newspapers and magazines. Companies were obsessed with creating human firewalls, a collection of employees who so thoroughly understood cybersecurity that they could prevent most attacks.

At the time (and likely still today), very few companies had a human firewall. A large percentage of companies don't even employ cybersecurity best practices. Those that do often merely send out a packet containing their policies to new hires and maybe host an online training seminar. The chief security information officers (CISOs) and VPs of IT security, the people responsible for protecting a company, never actually know how much training each hire internalizes. Many hires barely open the cybersecurity training documents and typically forget everything they learn the next day. Not because they're lazy, but because they're busy doing what the company hired them to.

These lapses in knowledge can lead to cataclysmic breakdowns. In 2016, the Hillary Clinton campaign suffered a hack because somebody replied to a phishing scheme. And in 2021, the Colonial Pipeline was completely shut down because one employee reused an old password that was easily stolen. Such breakdowns were even more common in the almost six years I worked at PentaSafe. CISO and VPs of IT security were terrified of a similar attack crippling their systems.

At the time, PentaSafe had a Skunk Works project in development that would help companies train employees on how to protect against cyberattacks. It created a single platform that held security policy documents and training videos, which all employees could access. The company could create and assign small tests in the platform to get proof that employees understood the training and to see if there were gaps in employees' knowledge. If there were, the company could provide additional training.

Our CEO asked me if I thought we should bring this product to market. He wondered if we should axe the project because he wasn't sure that it would sell. I could tell that the software platform would never become our top-selling product because it wasn't a must-have. It was more of a should-have. Most companies agreed they should do a better job training their employees, but that rarely made it a top priority.

I saw the product as a huge opportunity to differentiate our company. Even though the tool itself wasn't a must-have, it addressed a hot-button, top-of-mind, should-solve problem—a wedge problem. I figured that if we went all in on the human firewall angle in our marketing, we could draw a lot of attention and use this product as a wedge to get us in the door. We would produce a lot of leads, build relationships with prospects, and ultimately sell them our other products.

We launched the Skunk Works product. To market it, we created the Security Awareness Index, an online assessment that told prospects how well their employees understood their security policies. It gave each company a grade (A–F) and showed how they compared to their peers. We led most of our marketing with this free assessment and the associated content we created about it.

It worked. And I was right—we didn't sell much of the security policy testing and training platform. They'd already received value from us through our assessment that outlined their vulnerabilities. They could develop and deploy their own training programs to reduce the risks. But the assessment started a conversation with prospects. Then we would have our salespeople ask, "So, what really keeps you up at night?" They would share the problems they needed to solve, and we got to show them how our core products would make their issues disappear. More often than not, they bought.

Build Ideal Buyer Personas

Once you know who you are targeting and their must-solve problems, you can put together an ideal buyer persona that details the types of people who will be making purchasing decisions about your product. The personas illuminate the context of the customers' world, so you can communicate with them effectively. When building personas, use every scrap of information you can about your customers, including digital data gathering; case study interviews; customer interactions; and conversations with analysts, salespeople, and customer service personnel. The more detailed and fleshed out the persona, the better. A buyer persona includes five parts: background, hangouts, challenges, goals, and purchasing role.

Background

This is the demographic and psychographic data. How old are they? What is their job title? What sort of company do they work for? What size? What do they want? What are their personal aspirations? For example, Robert, thirty-seven, is the director of IT security and leads a team of thirty IT security professionals. He lives in San Francisco, California, and has a computer science degree. He is a first-time director, new to his company, and wants to make his mark quickly.

Hangouts

The hangouts part describes where they spend the most time, both online and off-line. This knowledge will help you place advertisements and content that reaches the right prospects. For example, Robert regularly attends IT security trade shows and participates in user group meetings for key technologies like Oracle and Microsoft. He follows industry influencers and analysts and participates in online forums.

Challenges

This part is usually where you would write in the buyer's must-solve problems. Steer away from generic challenges. You can't build a marketing campaign based on, the customer's desire to grow their business but cut costs. Everyone has that problem. You need to get more specific. For example, Robert worries that his organization is at risk of a cyberattack because people are lax about IT security. He often feels like he's the lone voice constantly sounding the alarm, and regularly thinks about ways to reduce his company's risk. Regulators just released new compliance requirements for his industry, and he needs to quickly make changes to pass the next round of audits.

Goals

What specifically does your target buyer want? Personally? Professionally? For example, Robert is regularly looking for new or better ways to educate people on IT security policy awareness and compliance. But because he is new to the organization, he needs to gain buy-in for his ideas and offer a strong business case to encourage his organization to change.

Purchasing Role

How much budget does your ideal target buyer have? Can they make buying decisions on their own, or do they need approval from above? For example, Robert has a budget of $5 million dollars and is the ultimate decision maker for IT purchases under $100K. For anything over that amount, he needs to get sign-off from his VP and CTO.

Remember that in the B2B world, most companies make buying decisions by committee. The larger the company, the more people involved. As you move upmarket, you will need to develop new buyer personas. That's what happened while I worked for Thycotic. At first we targeted midsize companies and only had to convince CISOs and possibly an IT leader to buy our product. When we targeted larger companies, we needed to convince people all over the organization, including the legal team, the COO, and systems administrators. As we grew, we developed a specific persona for every single possible buyer and influencer that we targeted.

These target personas dictate huge segments of strategy. For instance, if you know that you're targeting younger people, you might invest more in Instagram ads than in LinkedIn ads. If you target twenty-something IT staff at tech start-ups but produce content that sounds like it was written for a fifty-year-old IBM exec, you won't make a lot of sales. All of this contributes to velocity because you can streamline the process as much as possible and target people by speaking to them the way they want to be spoken to.

Craft a Killer Value Proposition

Once you understand your ideal buyer and their must-solve problems, you need messaging that quickly connects with them. To do this, you need a killer value proposition. A value proposition promises value to a customer. It tells customers exactly why they should buy from you as opposed to someone else.

An excellent value proposition will provide a massive boost. If I could give you only one piece of advice to improve conversions on your website, it would be to make sure your value propositions quickly resonate with target buyers. To create a killer value proposition, follow two rules: focus on benefits and value, not bits and bytes, and be specific.

Focus on Benefits and Value, Not Bits and Bytes

Keep in mind that your value proposition is written for the people you're targeting to do business with. It's crucial that your value propositions focus on what the buyer needs, not on what you, the seller, care about. In the tech industry, I call this bits and bytes value propositions. Weak value propositions emphasize features and functionality rather than the benefits and value buyers are seeking. Benefits are the advantages the product offers. The value is how those benefits support the buyer's underlying goals.

Trust me, no one cares that your product is built on a cloud-native architecture. That won't drive more customer interest. Your customers need to know *why* that cloud architecture matters and how that benefits them. For example, cloud-native architecture could mean a more secure, scalable product, or a product that takes less effort to maintain.

But the best value propositions don't stop at benefits; they address the value. Connect the benefit the product offers directly to the impact it will make on their company. To return to the prior example, customers gain value from cloud-native architecture because they don't need to worry about increasing their capacity when they grow, ongoing maintenance work, or having to apply security patches. They save money and time. Ultimately, they reach return on their investment faster than they would without using cloud-native architecture. If you can make that value-packed case to a customer, you have a better chance of closing a sale.

Be Specific

The best value propositions zero in on your niche and the buyer's must-solve problem. To do that, value propositions must be loaded with specifics. At minimum, a great value proposition contains these three things:

1. *Who* benefits from your products
2. *How* you help customers overcome challenges and meet their goals
3. *Why* your product or approach is different and better than anyone else's

Ideally, you'll want to choose details that differentiate you from the competition. But keep in mind that anything you include in your value proposition must be relevant to the target audience, true, and provable. On top of that, the value proposition must be clear. Make sure that someone can read and understand the proposition in about five seconds.

A generic, bland, or opaque value proposition dies on the page. As an example, let's dissect a value proposition that needs some love.

TAKE 1: *"We improve the quality of education."*

This could be any education company, right? We don't know what type of people this company helps or what specific help people receive. The word *quality* sounds like something good for customers, but it doesn't tell them exactly what *quality* means or how they should measure it.

Let's add some specifics.

TAKE 2: *"We provide a comprehensive library of easy-to-manage, personalized video-based learning tools for K–12 schools."*

Now the value proposition includes:

- who the customers are: K–12 schools
- what the company provides: video-based learning
- what the competitive differentiator is: we can assume similar tools aren't as easy to use

This is better but still too weak to influence anyone. It doesn't explain why customers should care about this approach or why they should buy from this particular company. It doesn't ignite a spark. When we add even more details, we get a value proposition that pops.

TAKE 3: *"We empower K–12 teachers to help students become active learners. Our easy-to-use video-based learning tools boost student engagement fivefold. We're the only video solution that adapts to a student's specific learning challenges."*

Now the buyer knows the following:

- what benefits to expect: students become active learners
- how we can measure this: engagement increases fivefold
- why this company: we don't have to guess at the competitive differentiators, the company tells us why it's better than the competition; it's easy, and, most importantly, it adapts to the needs of different students

More Than a Slogan

Once you settle on a value proposition, that should become a North Star for your entire business. Simply put, if your messaging doesn't align with your actions, it torpedoes your credibility with customers. They will feel bamboozled and almost always go somewhere else. When you combine a killer value proposition that is supported by totally aligned actions across an organization, you have an excellent chance to succeed compared to your competitors.

At Thycotic, the value proposition that I landed on was that we were faster, easier, and more affordable than the competition. In other words, our major selling point became simplicity. That meant that our company's guiding tenet also became simplicity. We weren't just selling the simplicity of our products, but the deep simplicity that comes from every way a customer interacts with the business.

The senior leadership rallied everyone to the cause of simplicity and created a company-wide movement. At the core of the movement was a team that audited our entire processes, making them as intuitive and user-friendly as possible. Then we looked across every function. We rooted out such things as complexity in contracts, pricing, marketing, and the way customers interact with support.

Making our organization as user-friendly as possible led to endless opportunities to create new content and marketing. Our content creators wrote about the simplicity of our products, our pricing, and our customer service practices. And, to the point, they kept all the content simple as well. We provided the sales team with charts that highlighted the key talking points about how, as one of our taglines put it, we provided "Cybersecurity products that make your life easier."

Of course, competitors adapt. After we had posted several consecutive successful quarters, our competitors swerved and tried to claim that *they* offered the simplest solution. However, most of them hadn't done the actual legwork to back up that claim. One competitor leaned particularly hard into the simplicity angle. When it did, I happened to get a copy of its user manual, which had well over one thousand pages. Ours had about thirty. We used this discrepancy to prove how much simpler our solution was. The competitor's user manual was so long that had it been a novel, it would have been one of the longest ever written. So I made a printout for our sales team to share with prospects of the longest books ever. Our competitor's user manual ranked right up there with *In Search of Lost Time* and *Clarissa, or, the History of a Young Lady*. I gave our sales reps a picture of the table of contents of our competitor's one thousand–page user manual and our thirty-page user manual. In sales conversations, they showed both to prospects and per-fectly encapsulated the difference between the two companies by asking one profound question: "Which user manual do you want to read?"

The prospects would laugh, but they understood the point—they never doubted which product was easier to use. It all worked. Even though our competitor was much larger, we established a foothold in the market. We won several customers that otherwise would have gone to the competitor, who didn't know what hit them.

CHAPTER 2

Build Content That Buyers Need Now

At the heart of every digital marketing strategy is content. It does the heavy lifting. It *is* the campaign and how your organization sells itself to the world. Content marketing is the bridge that connects consumers to the brands they like. In short, content is one of, if not *the*, most important part of HVDM. The difference between a slow and a HVDM approach comes down to the perceived value of your content to target buyers. A great blog post, free tool, or video will generate leads and revenue for years after it goes live.

Most organizations struggle to generate revenue with their content. Some buy into one of the most pervasive marketing fallacies, the old Don Draper style of advertising that uses slick and clever content to convince someone to buy a product. But you can't make someone buy, and you can't outwit customers. Especially not with the rise of the internet, as buyers can easily do their research online and become better informed.

Some organizations fail to realize the importance of their content, and potential buyers can sniff out poor content incredibly fast. They won't tell you your content sucks, but they will quickly move on. Great content offers value and meaning. It gives people an entire ecosystem to tap into for information and guidance, and to learn how they and their business benefit from your services and products.

The secret is to create content that educates potential buyers about how to think about their problem, offers potential solutions, and then demonstrates the benefits of your solution. In other words, create content that quickly offers real value. Ideally, you want to provide target buyers with information so valuable that they will share it with their peers, colleagues, and bosses. If they do that, your authority with key decision makers will be established.

Few companies manage to build content that provides real value. They mostly generate content that benefits them, more than their prospects. That kills the website visitor-to-lead conversion rate and sales velocity. People don't have time to read content that waxes poetic. They read what they need to in order to do their jobs, achieve high-priority objectives, and benefit personally and professionally. To create content that buyers covet, start by building a content marketing strategy. Then you can move to creating the content itself.

Build a Content Marketing Strategy

There are myriad types of content to choose from:

- Blog posts
- Social posts
- White papers
- E-books
- Infographics
- Live events

- Case studies
- Podcasts
- Web pages
- Demos
- Online tools
- Webinars
- Newsletters
- Interactive videos
- Guides
- Games
- Data visuals
- Courses
- Animations
- SMS and push notifications

Don't waste time trying to create as much content across as many media as possible. Instead, be intentional about the content you create and generate pieces that help achieve a specific goal. That goal will vary from piece to piece, but two overarching goals are to give a view of the unique value your company provides and to help generate pipeline and revenue. To achieve success with both goals, you need two different kinds of content, what I call foundational content and the core content. These two types of content are intricately interconnected. The foundational content helps build trust, establishes authority, and differentiates your company from competitors, and the core content communicates the unique value of your products and services.

Foundational Content

Foundational content is just about anything that does not directly lead to sales and revenue, such as your website's "About Us" page, the "Leadership Team" page, the "FAQ" page, and the "Customer Support" page. Make sure that these pages create a cohesive vision of your company that aligns with your unique value proposition. Everything on your website is an opportunity to influence how a prospect feels about your company—don't let it go to waste.

Consider creating professionally shot "our culture" videos. These tools serve two major purposes: they can help recruit top talent by showcasing your workplace culture and approach, and they can help introduce your company to potential buyers. In the B2B space, the most effective customer-provider relationships are actual partnerships. By introducing prospects to your company, philosophy, and way of doing business, you can show buyers how your company would be an excellent partner.

Core Content

Once you have the foundational content in place, you can move on to the core content. The core content educates a buyer about how your products and services will uniquely help them solve their problem and add value.

I break core content into two broad categories: ungated and gated. Ungated content is anything that the prospect can access just by clicking through a web page such as blog posts, articles, and product data sheets. Ungated content gives people your company's background and solutions and offers them quick ways to see what sets you apart. But it's the gated content that produces leads and contributes the most to revenue. Gated content is the longer form content that offers real value such as white papers, free tools, and product trials. To get gated content, prospects fill out a lead form that asks for their name, company, job title, and contact information. This data is used for lead scoring (more on this in chapter six) to determine whether the prospect is likely to buy.

To judge the quality of core content, ask yourself whether a prospect would pay five dollars to access your gated content. That might seem like too much to ask, but it's not. Most people will only offer up their personal information to receive something they absolutely want or need. For a more quantitative way to measure quality, look at the website visitor-to-lead conversion rate.

When I was CMO at Thycotic, we grew the number of visitors coming to our website every month for six years. At the same time, our website visitor-to-lead conversion rate was consistently over 5 percent. This meant that our content was so strong, that 5 percent of all visitors willingly gave us their personal information. Think about this for a moment. How often do you give up your personal information online? If you're like me, the answer is almost never.

To know what sort of content to create, rely on metrics and conversations with real customers. Pay attention to what creates the most conversions, clicks, leads, opportunities, and revenue. In addition, make sure that you know exactly how prospects prefer to consume your content. For example, do they prefer mobile sites or downloadable white papers? Videos or podcasts? While the metrics can reveal these preferences, sometimes you just need to ask prospects what they prefer. All of this will help maximize successful results. But the real key to success is to design content for each step in the buyer's journey.

Design Content for Each Step in the Buyer's Journey

As a buyer considers their options, they move through phases of the buyer's journey. At each phase they have different levels of knowledge and different needs. When you're creating content, your primary objective is to connect with your target audience no matter where they are in the buyer's journey. The four stages of the buyer's journey are discover, consider, evaluate, and purchase.

1. **Discover:** The buyer has a problem but often cannot articulate it. Focus on educational content that helps buyers define and gain clarity on their problem. For example, a white paper in which an expert discusses common customer problems, or an educational webinar.

2. **Consider:** Once the buyer defines their problem in more detail, they're ready to consider options to solve it. Focus on content that goes into more detail on the problem and discusses the best way(s) for solving it. For example, offer free tools that help customers diagnose the nature and extent of their problems, and tools that show how your product could help.

3. **Evaluate:** The buyer evaluates specific solutions as they decide on the right company to buy from. Focus on content that shows why you offer the best solution. For example, product trials, customer testimonials, or case studies.

4. **Purchase:** The buyer becomes a customer. Focus on reinforcing their purchase decision and providing guidelines on how to use the product. For example, product usage videos.

A content gap at any of the four stages takes the velocity out of HVDM. It prevents companies from connecting with buyers and fails to lead them through the sales cycle. When I took over at Thycotic, we lacked content at almost every stage of the journey. Most of the early success came from the company's excellence at trade shows, referrals, and other similar approaches. While valuable, these strategies are far more difficult and expensive to scale than HVDM. As soon as I became CMO, we pivoted to creating content for each stage of the buyer's journey.

To do that, I first needed to understand the landscape we operated in, our product, how we compared to our competitors, and our customers' must-solve and top-of-mind issues. Thycotic was a relatively small start-up, going against much larger competitors. I quickly found a wedge issue that I could use to break into the market.

When I started with Thycotic, a major issue, frequently in the news, was the proliferation of passwords through most companies' digital infrastructure. As companies bought new pieces of hardware and software and expanded to a cloud infrastructure, they also acquired new passwords for every device. Most people don't realize this, but every single piece of technology, and each piece of software, has its own default password.

These passwords gave hackers the keys to the kingdom. If they found the default password for a server, computer, or cloud system, for example, then they could enter the system and access whatever they wanted. This is called a privileged password attack, and it got a lot of buzz in the cybersecurity world. CISOs and VPs of IT security wanted to secure their systems against such attacks. Most also recognized that they didn't understand the full extent of the threat.

They bought new computers, smartphones, and tablets. Some companies downloaded new software, then changed software, then changed back. Everyone had email and access to several applications. Some changed cloud carriers a few times or kept multiple cloud carriers. In some cases, the marketing team used Macs, while the rest of the company used Dell PCs. And, of course, on top of all of this, some employees still used their personal computers and their personal cell phones. In short, most companies suddenly had massive networks and an enormous number of devices to secure. Most CISOs couldn't track all the moving parts, let alone all the privileged passwords.

I realized that this was our wedge, we just needed the right content to connect to people and get us leads. One part of our privileged password management software allowed companies to diagnose their vulnerabilities by showing them the privileged passwords that actually existed. I asked the R&D department to carve the discovery functionality off from the rest of our product and package it as a free tool we could use in our marketing. They did, and we ended up with the Privileged Password Discovery Tool, which became one of our most successful pieces of content. It responded to a pressing issue and generated tons of great leads.

IT security professionals couldn't download it fast enough. Most of them realized that they needed to shore up their security, and if they wanted to do that quickly, they needed our software. That realization primed them for sales. After a prospect used this free tool, our salespeople could reach out and just be helpful. They might say, "So, how many privileged passwords did you find? That's a lot. Do you think you can manage and secure those on your own? Would you like to learn about how our products might help you solve this quickly and forever?"

As great as this tool was on its own, it would not have been enough to build true velocity. It only captured the imagination of people who already knew about the risks privileged passwords pose—those in the consider phase. Most of our visitors were in the discover phase. Some prospects weren't even aware of what privileged passwords were and the risks they present. For them, we created educational content, like white papers and blog posts that defined privileged passwords. But we made sure at each stage to address our wedge issue. We wanted to prime them to understand the value of the free tool once they reached that part of the process.

Even if they were in the consider phase when they found us, the tool alone might not have been enough to get them to purchase. They might use it and completely understand the extent of their problem but remain unconvinced that we could help them solve it. They wanted to see our actual product in action. We produced content that allowed them to do that—a thirty-day free trial with supporting content that explained how to use the software. Our content told a cohesive story about what privileged password attacks were, how companies were vulnerable to them, and how we could reduce that risk. We backed this up with content that provided overwhelming third-party validation from customers and analysts. All of this, together with extensive sales training, created velocity.

The Content Creation Process

In my career, I found that the only way to consistently create great content is to have a highly efficient process in place to help manage all the content produced. At Thycotic, we treated our content production as if we were running the *New Yorker*. We planned out an editorial calendar at least a quarter in advance. The calendar included daily tasks for each team member. Then we had weekly production meetings, where all the writers, graphic and web designers, and video creators gathered to report on their progress. From there, we could take course corrections, make updates, answer questions, and confirm that everything was on schedule.

Every company's content creation process will look different, but I have found two things that will ensure excellent content every time: brainstorm new ideas with the best and brightest and tell content stories to connect quickly with buyers.

Brainstorm Content with the Best and Brightest

I've seen far too many CMOs take a laissez-faire approach to content development. They might hire a few writers, a video team, and some graphic designers and trust them to create a lot of content. In my experience, the best content comes from a more rigorous process.

My process emphasizes cross-functional collaboration. Twice a year when I worked at Thycotic, I would pull the smartest people from various departments, such as R&D leaders, the best sales engineers, top salespeople, and top product management and professional services personnel, who understood either our products or our customers. I sent everyone examples of excellent content, mostly from businesses in other industries. Then I convened a brainstorming meeting and asked each person to share one or two ideas that they thought would resonate with customers. We decided as a team which would provide the most value and developed our favorites.

This meeting generated much of our highest-performing content, including Thycotic's Privileged Account Management (PAM) Maturity Model. The PAM Maturity Model essentially broke down the various stages of maturity that a company's PAM processes might go through. Before the model, our prospects had no way to tell if they were PAM laggards or leaders. We knew that they wanted to know what great PAM security looked like and how to get there. The PAM Maturity Model taught them both.

To maximize velocity, we repurposed the model into several types of content. We wrote articles, gave webinars, and produced videos about it. We developed an online assessment so people could see where they stood in the maturity model. We built free tools that specifically responded to the model, and we also used the language of the model in our free trials and demos. Our salespeople learned to use the model's language in their conversations with customers. This all shortened our sales cycle. It trained customers to think about PAM in the same way as industry experts and our salespeople. Everyone spoke the same language. The sales team knew exactly how the customer thought about PAM and could explain how Thycotic would help them reach higher levels of maturity.

The ideas from these meetings became my top priority in budget allocation. The best ideas can't move the needle if they don't come to fruition. If we came up with a new free tool that we needed to build, I would offer someone on the R&D team extra money to develop it for us over the weekend. If we couldn't do things in-house, we would hire independent contractors to develop what we needed.

To create Thycotic's PAM Maturity Model, for example, we enlisted a team of experts and writers. Led by an experienced product marketer, they drafted and refined the model to ensure it was both valuable and credible. We didn't want it to appear biased or to be judged by prospects as marketing fluff. If either occurred, it would have failed. Prospects would have dismissed it as simplistic or ignored it as a marketing gimmick. We kept the model honest and straightforward. We highlighted how our products could help but acknowledged our limitations.

Because we invested so much time to making the model excellent, it showed real staying power. As of this writing, the maturity model continues to be a high-performing marketing tactic. This underscores an important point: great content has a longer shelf life than most marketers realize. If something works, don't go away from it. Trust me, the entire target audience has not seen that content. It might seem like old hat to you, but to first-time visitors to your web page, it is still new and groundbreaking. Make updates, of course, and continue to think of ways to repurpose existing content. But don't throw out your best ideas just because you think that newer ones might be better.

This is just one example. Each brainstorming session would usually produce more ideas than we could ever use. I was never at a loss for great content or forced to live with an irregular trickle of boring blog posts. This process had one other great advantage: it created a built-in team of dedicated cheerleaders for the pieces of content we developed. The best ideas usually came from leaders in different departments who worked hard on them. They cared about the content and promoted the ideas. They would tell their peers and networks about it. All of this served as a force multiplier and helped us grow with lightning speed in our market.

Connect to Buyers Through Stories

Humans use stories as mental shortcuts to understand the world. In most established industries, several companies offer similar products. Often, this leads buyers to settle on the product with the most compelling story. To ensure that you create compelling stories, follow these five rules: find a great hook, keep it concise, make it personal, say something unique, and show, don't tell.

1. **Find a Great Hook:** Online, you have seconds to intrigue and attract a potential buyer to your content. Find an excellent hook and use it to hold their attention. Put it in the headline.

2. **Keep It Concise:** No potential buyer wants to read your company's version of *War and Peace*. People on the internet jump from page to page and skim. They stick around only if something stands out and feels like a manageable read. They need to see the value of the information, and your value proposition, right away.

3. **Make It Personal:** Effective stories draw on our emotions. You can do the same with your content. It's not just about capturing buyers' attention; it's about capturing their imagination. I'm not saying that you need to include an anecdote or long narrative in each piece of content. What matters is that you provide insights into the pressures that buyers face. Connect with their goals. Entice them with the real benefits your solution offers. Provide value to the reader—a bit of information that helps them better understand their world. Above all, focus your story on them—not on you.

4. **Say Something Unique:** Your content will never hold your visitors' attention if you regurgitate the same talking points as everyone else in the industry. You need to find a unique angle, ideally one that aligns with what differentiates your company or your products.

For example, while I worked at PentaSafe, we sold cybersecurity software that was similar to what our competitors offered. One key differentiator, however, was that we offered a unique product that helped ensure our customers' employees understand their company's security policies. To market this, we created a Security Awareness Index. We offered a free assessment that helped organizations learn if their employees understood their security policies, a key part of defending against cyberattacks. This grabbed people's attention because they quickly learned whether their company was at risk and the magnitude of that risk. Through this, we not only elevated their awareness, but we also built trust around our unique approach to solving urgent problems. Once prospects realized that we understood their problems, we could differentiate the value of our solution and position ourselves as the perfect partner.

5. **Show, Don't Tell:** Telling people that "our solution performs well" doesn't entice buyers. In my career, we always made sure to *show* the actual improvements. In content, describe how a product changes a customer's life. Go into detail. Provide data and facts that back up your assertions. This is even more effective when you can get existing customers to do the showing for you through content like customer success stories and videos.

CHAPTER 3

Master Google

Think about it: when you decide to buy something and want to research it first, where do you go? You go to Google. You're not alone, with 62 percent of B2B buyers saying they develop selection criteria for finalizing a vendor list based solely on digital content. And Google accounts for 76 percent of global internet searches,* making it the most popular tool by a wide margin for accessing digital content. If your HVDM program is to be successful, you must be visible on Google.

People will typically reach your website from Google in one of two ways: either by clicking an ad you paid for or by performing a search where your business comes up naturally, which is called organic traffic. Overall, B2B companies generate twice as much revenue from organic searches than

---

* Ogi Djuraskovic, "Google Search Statistics and Facts 2022 (You Must Know)," *FirstSiteGuide* (blog), January 10, 2022, https://firstsiteguide.com/google-search-stats/.

any other channel.* This occurs because searchers trust organic links more than paid links, thinking that organic links earned rather than bought their way to the top position. Best of all, organic traffic costs are nominal outside of the time and money invested in web and content development. For that reason, the bulk of this chapter will cover how to rank organically in Google. Google Ads also plays an important role in the success of a HVDM strategy, which I will cover later.

To be found organically, your business must show up near the top of the search engine results pages (SERPs)—the pages that show up when someone makes a query online. Ranking high in the SERPs takes effort. A Google search may yield over a billion results, yet fewer than thirty of those will show up on page one. Google decides which pages deserve to rank. To be among the most deserving, you need to master a process known as search engine optimization (SEO).

Generate Organic Traffic with SEO

ORGANIC TRAFFIC

SEO is a complicated practice, but, simply put, it helps search engines understand your content and deliver it to the right people—the ones who want it.

---

* "Organic Search Improves Ability to Map to Consumer Intent," BrightEdge Research, accessed January 19, 2022, https://videos.brightedge.com/research-report/BrightEdge_ChannelReport2019_FINAL.pdf.

It takes a lot of planning and time to bear fruit. It is not a quick fix but rather an ongoing strategy of regular content releases. The chart on page 44 shows the SEO benchmarks that I use to evaluate success. A company that starts to seriously work on SEO tomorrow might see only a small percentage of their traffic come from organic searches. It almost always takes over a year to even get to the good range (35–50 percent), and much longer than that to reach great (50 percent and over).

For that reason, it is imperative to start thinking about SEO as early as possible. Don't wait until your website goes live to plan an SEO strategy. Too many companies don't even budget for SEO and end up scrambling to put together a strategy with limited resources. I always made SEO a top priority budget item. I hired the best specialists I could and incorporated their input at every phase of the marketing process.

SEO is as much art as it is science. Google doesn't share its full ranking algorithms, so there will always be factors that SEO experts will never know. So while it is possible to tackle SEO by yourself, I recommend hiring an SEO specialist or agency to work in close concert with your team. Like anything else in life, the more you put into SEO, the more you get out. Don't expect to just hire someone and forget about the entire process. During my career, I went so far as to hold two people accountable for our success on Google: my SEO expert and my webmaster. They were the two people with the most direct control over SEO. The SEO expert handled the front end of SEO, like planning and optimizing the content. The webmaster handled the back end. They tagged the content with the right metadata and keywords and maintained the website. Google wants to deliver the most relevant information paired with the most pleasant user experience. The webmaster must create that seamless experience.

In the next chapter, I discuss at length how a webmaster does that. For now, we will focus on the front-facing end. Here, I will explain the basics of SEO. This will give you enough of an overview to take the first few SEO steps on your own and to understand how to effectively collaborate with an SEO expert, whether that be somebody you hire internally or an outside agency. These basics are to understand page one of SERPs, identify your ideal keywords, optimize your content, and earn backlinks.

Understand Page One of SERPs

A Google search generates pages populated with different types of results, depending on the phrasing of the query. They include:

- text ads at the top and bottom of the page.
- image ads—ads with photographs.
- a featured snippet—a listing where a snippet describing the page comes before a link to the page.
- videos.
- Google My Business listings—businesses that show up with a Google map and have a View All option to expand the list.
- questions and answers—often under the heading of "People Also Ask." Be aware that when you click on one of these questions, your action prompts more questions to appear thereby pushing other organic listings farther down the page.
- no-click results—those that answer the query without the searcher having to click through to the website that provided the answer.
- a variety of web pages and blog posts.
- popular products, usually with photographs.
- related searches and other popular search queries.

Aside from the ads, everything above is an organic listing. The best organic listings are the links that lead directly to a web page or blog. In a certain sense, all the rest is clutter. People who visit a web page from organic listings convert to leads much more frequently than those who skim the no-click results or follow a YouTube link.

In the early days of Google, almost every search would show four or five direct-link organic listings in one screen. As of this writing, most searches yield three ads before the first organic result. The average number of direct-link listings on the first screen (which always receive the most clicks) has dropped from five to three. And that's before you account for any of the clutter. While the previous types of results will change as Google tests new features, the general trend has been to add more clutter. To get the best results in your SEO, you need to make sure that you can be found through the clutter.

That being said, this change created an opportunity: each type of result provides a chance to get your company in front of potential customers, even if the link doesn't lead straight to your web page. The best SEO strategies create content that fits into each of the listed categories. A well-maintained YouTube page will make sure that your videos show up in searches. Content that answers direct questions will help you show up in questions-and-answers and no-click results. Pay attention to any change Google makes to page one of the SERPs, and then develop content that will rank for each new type of result.

Identify Your Ideal Keywords

People use keywords to search online. To attract customers through Google, companies must first understand exactly what keywords customers search for and which ones enable them to rank high in the SERPs. To start, you should understand what types of keywords exist. There are three categories of keywords:

1. **Head terms, or broad keywords:** Single keywords that offer no clues as to what the person really wants to know. For head term searches, Google will often deliver definitions and Wikipedia entries. Some examples include *software, insurance, T-shirts, task management,* and *passwords.*

2. **Short-tail keywords:** two- to three-word phrases that indicate what the person is looking for. These are often extremely competitive phrases such as *project management software, health insurance quote, promotional T-shirts, task management platform,* and *password security software.* Setting your sights on only short-tail keywords can set you up for failure.

3. **Long-tail keywords:** Descriptive phrases that contain four or more words such as *construction project management software for subcontractors, group insurance quote small business, promotional T-shirts with embroidered logos, centralized task management platform for teams, what's the best password security software for small to medium businesses.* These are by far the easiest keywords to rank in, and they bring the best traffic to your site.

At the same time, well-optimized web pages typically include a mix of all three types of keywords, though the most important of the three are long-tail keywords because they identify exactly what someone is looking for. For example, if you own a project management software company, it would take years to rank for *software,* and if you ever did, it would offer minimal payoff. Who's to say the searcher wants project management software and not photo-editing tools, or just general information about software?

Keywords such as *project management software* are better. But on Google, those keywords returns over 2 billion results! Something like *construction project management software for subcontractors* returns far fewer results.

These keywords also happen to be popular as people are searching for more and more specific data.

To discover what your audience searches for, I recommend using a paid tool that tracks monthly search volume. But search volume can't be the only criteria. Focus on keywords that show some sort of intent to buy. Words like *best privileged access management solutions* show far more intent than just *privileged access management software*. Then build content that will rank for those keywords and pay attention to the metrics. How many clicks do you get from that content? How much revenue does organic traffic from those searches generate? Through this research, you can create and consistently update a list of ideal keywords that you can work from to build out the rest of your website and internet capability.

At Thycotic, we used a spreadsheet to map relevant keywords to our current (and future) content. I also like to group similar keywords to create a theme for a page of content. That way you can create content that addresses the topic in-depth, which will rank for a family of keywords. In addition to that spreadsheet, I created a list I called my coveted keywords. These were the best of the best keywords, the searches that showed the absolute most intent to buy our products, such as *best PAM solution for financial services companies*. You don't search that unless you're in the market for new PAM software. I obsessed over these. I wanted to know each day where Thycotic ranked for each coveted keyword, and where our top three competitors ranked. We did everything we could to be in the top three results for these lists. If we started to dip, I instantly invested in new content, pages, and strategies related to those words.

Bear in mind that your SEO specialist cannot guarantee you'll rank for every keyword you set your heart on without resorting to questionable practices. If they make that promise, it is a red flag. A good SEO adviser will manage your expectations by explaining why you may not rank for certain keywords and help you choose more suitable ones.

Listen to your SEO specialist's advice. While you might think that it really matters to rank high in the SERPs for a broad term like *cybersecurity software*, in reality you'll get more satisfying results from more targeted keywords. A broad term might move the needle, if you succeed, but only to draw more traffic to your website, not necessarily to generate more leads that convert into revenue. And that's a big *if.* For those sorts of broad inquiries, Google heavily favors ads. As of this writing, a search for *cybersecurity software* returns only ads in the first screen. A good SEO expert will steer you away from an approach that is too broad. And if the broad keyword is that important to you, consider bidding for the word in a Google Ads campaign.

Understanding which keywords generate the most revenue by consistently tracking performance and testing new paths will prove invaluable. If, for example, I saw that we ranked high in a keyword we thought would generate a lot of traffic but didn't receive clicks of leads, then I would know to pivot content production away from that keyword. Additionally, as a marketing leader, you should always be able to explain why you have invested in ranking for the keywords that you used.

As the CMO, I regularly sat in board meetings, and some member, eager to prove a point, would grab a keyword that was in some way related to our business and Google it. Then they'd demand to know why our business doesn't rank at the top of the first page for that keyword. If this happens to you and you haven't prepared, and don't have clear data to justify why you have chosen to focus on the keywords that you have, then you might be in trouble. However, if you've done your homework, you will be able to justify the current strategy and prove how it generates more revenue at a lower cost.

Finally, there are a couple of common pitfalls to avoid. First, some companies try to game the system by hiding keywords in their content, for example, by making keywords the same color as the background of the web page so only the search engine can see them. Such practices if discovered by Google will result in a steep drop in the SERP rankings of these pages.

Second, companies may unknowingly cannibalize their keywords. In other words, they target the same keyword on ten different pages of their website or blog. This is a waste of time and money. Google will rank two pages at most, so it's better to focus on expanding your topics and making the pages you have as strong as possible.

Google My Business Page

The fastest and easiest way to feature in the SERPs with a few key searches is to claim and then fully develop your Google My Business page. Whereas most SEO processes take time to bear fruit, a business can go from no presence whatsoever, to the top of the organic results in two weeks by completing its Google My Business page. These pages show up, not only when people search for a company by name, but also when they search for location-related products or services—for example, *accountants in Philadelphia* or *software development company near me.*

While this might seem obvious, a surprising number of companies botch it. There are two common mistakes they make. First, they don't realize Google has sometimes already generated a Google My Business page for them, so they create and optimize a new page. But since Google already created a page, nobody sees the new, optimized page. The way to avoid this is simple: search your business and see if there is already a page. If there isn't, create one. If there is, then claim the page. Make sure to use a company email that you will always have access to, for example, marketing@companyname.com. If you let the employee you delegated the task to use their personal email, you will lose access to the account when they leave. Also, when adding your business name in Google My Business, you may make your business name describe the business. For example, if your company's legal name is John Smith and Partners, feel free to use John Smith and Partners Tax Accountants.

The second mistake companies make is to not fully complete or use their Google My Business listing. To maximize the power of your listing, complete all the fields available to you. Don't cut corners. Then write a thorough business description that includes keywords that describe what you do. Once you have all your business details written out, store them in a spreadsheet so you can use the exact same information on other platforms.

Then to make yourself findable through business-category searches, select a primary category for your business and several secondary categories (you can have up to ten, providing they are entirely relevant to your business). If you use creative terminology to describe your business, you'll be better off using colloquial terms on Google. For instance, your aesthetics boutique should be listed in the beauty salon category if you want anyone to find you on Google. Go to bit.ly/skahan-5 for a list of 2022 available categories.

Finally, and this matters for your brand reputation, monitor your Google reviews. Acknowledge the positive ones and respond to the negative ones in a manner that provides the reviewer a better experience. Google takes reviews into account when ranking results, and, more importantly, customers make decisions based on the reviews. If you show up first on an SERP but everyone complains about your business and it doesn't seem like you care, then you will negatively impact future revenue.

Optimize Your Content

At its core, Google is an algorithm that attempts to think like a human. Anytime the engineers at Google tweak the search engine, they try to make searching more like conversing with another person than it was before. Keywords are the language that Google uses to conduct this conversation. When a human inputs a search term, they receive content that matches their query. The key to optimizing for Google is to make your content fit into that search-response conversation as easily as possible. Some pieces of content, like anything that answers a direct question, naturally fit into that flow better than others. But to excel at SEO, each piece of content should address a searcher's problem or concern. Some people churn out loads of content on whatever they feel like writing about. While this might be fun, it does little to improve SERP rankings or drive high-quality traffic. Start with a thorough understanding of what your prospects care about and will look for, and then mold the content based on that.

Once you have written the right content, you can optimize it. Remember Google ranks web pages, not websites. Therefore, each page represents an opportunity to rank for keywords. Of course, this only works if the page contains the keywords. To make sure that happens, SEO experts and content writers should meet twice: once before the writer drafts content and again before they publish. When the writer starts their first draft, they should discuss the topic with the SEO expert. The SEO expert can research ideal keywords for that content and give them to the writer. Then when the writer finishes the draft, the SEO expert can review it to make sure it is optimized for Google.

The SEO expert should verify that the writer used the full long-tail keywords appropriately and often in the title, the headers, the titles of any images or graphics, and at least a few times in the text. Content writers tend to shorten things. For example, they might write "our software solutions" instead of the keyword "our project management software solution." While it might seem wordy, it's clear and specific, which is a fundamental pillar of strong writing anyway. But exercise caution—content stuffed with repetitive keywords comes across as impersonal and boring.

The keywords should match the content. To rank in the SERPs, every page doesn't need killer content, aggressive calls to action, or long text. But every page must fulfill the expectations of the viewer. Don't try to optimize all your web pages using your desirable keywords list. For example, the keyword ranking for your "Leadership" page is the common sense query "[your company name] leadership"; your "Contact Us" page should rank for "[your company name] contact information." Then deliver content that solves the query. Don't bait searchers seeking a how-to solution, then offer them little more than a sales pitch.

The SEO expert should also make sure that the content uses plain, direct language organized in an intuitive manner. The Google algorithm scans for headers and paragraph breaks to make sure that a page doesn't overwhelm with intimidating blocks of text. An SEO edit helps make sure that any article can be skimmed. People prefer it to complicated-sounding jargon anyway, and so does Google. Relatedly, SEO experts should make sure that content calls products and services what they are. That's what people will be looking for, not for a fancier term that only your company uses. Then SEO experts should make sure the content is long enough to rank. Of course, length alone will not propel a page to the top of the SERPs. Google rewards pages that contain lots of helpful information, and it uses article length as a metric to judge this. Articles shorter than three paragraphs rarely receive high rankings.

Earn Backlinks

Backlinks are links that point from a different website back to a specific web page on your website. If the backlink originates from a high-quality page, it counts as a valuable vote for that web page. The more high-quality backlinks, the more SEO value your page gains. High quality is the key here. A lot of people will offer to boost the number of backlinks to your page. But there's a high likelihood they'll provide links from questionable websites. This will tank your credibility with Google.

You must earn high-quality backlinks. Throughout my career, I accomplished this by building relationships with influencers in my field who then linked to our content from their pages. For example, while I worked for Thycotic, we published an article about the top cybersecurity bloggers. We didn't reach out to these bloggers beforehand, and we didn't beg them to link back to our content. Instead, we wrote an article that they would all want to share because it made them look good. After they shared it, we reached out to build relationships with the bloggers. Eventually, some of them guest-blogged for us, which they linked to from their websites. Suddenly, we were on their radar, and when they wrote articles, they occasionally referenced and backlinked to our content. This made us visible to the readers of those blogs while bolstering our authority and our rankings in SERPs.

Google Ads: Pay-per-Click (PPC) Advertising

Often, organic listings alone won't maximize your velocity. You will need to supplement with Google Ads. These ads can be powerful tools and enable you to:

- gain rapid visibility.
- reach people where they are. (In addition to the SERPS, Google Ads can appear on over two million websites,[*] reaching over 90 percent of people on the internet.[†])
- target your audiences by keyword, location, interests, age, gender, and other demographics.
- retarget people who've visited your site recently with ads based on what part of the site they visited.
- remarket to people who have purchased from you before, typically resulting in higher conversion rates.

---

[*] Lisa Raehsler, "The 8 Best PPC Ad Networks," SearchEngine Journal, February 10, 2021, https://www.searchenginejournal.com/ppc-guide/best-ppc-ad-networks/.

[†] Google, "About targeting for Display campaigns," Google Ads Help, accessed January 20, 2022, https://support.google.com/google-ads/answer/2404191?hl=en.

Small companies often try to save money and handle their own Google Ads. Some navigate the Google Ads dashboard, intuitively creating ads, adding keywords, and setting bid limits. Others choose Google's automated options, and yet others accept guidance from a Google representative.

None of these options, and I emphasize *none* of these options are good.

The likelihood you'll make a costly error, or several, is extremely high. The Google Ads platform is complex. Only experts with in-depth knowledge and experience with Google Ads paired with an understanding of your company can design campaigns that deliver a high return on investment. You can quickly waste far more money than you would spend on recruiting an ad campaign manager.

Of course, hire your campaign manager carefully. Require transparency. Don't settle for an all-in monthly fee—you must know how much of your budget goes toward clicks and how much toward campaign management. Also, require access to your Google Ads from your own Google account. Your agency may choose to access your ads by linking your account to their own dashboard, and that's normal. But avoid agencies that create your campaign in a separate platform that you have no access to—you'll lose your ads if you switch vendors.

I like to hire firms that can handle both my SEO and my Google Ads responsibilities because both strategies are intimately related. And as with SEO, you can't just hire a Google Ads agency and let it loose. In my experience, you should have a sense of your Google Ads budget and goals before you engage a firm.

Budgeting for Google Ads

The Google Ads platform is accommodating when it comes to budgets—you decide how much you want to spend per day, and Google ensures that come month's end you've stayed within your limit, although it may under or overspend on a day-to-day basis.

The average cost per click on Google is between $1 and $2 but this varies depending on industry, with law firms paying up to $100 per click. Some small businesses spend $500 a month on Google Ads, and several giant organizations spend well over $1 million each month.

I personally spend more on PPC ads than on traditional advertising, banner ads, and video ads. I find that among the paid ad options, PPCs generate by far the greatest return on investment. To decide how I allocate that budget, I simply track the metrics. Which keywords produced the most money for the lowest cost? The average midsize company spends between $9,000 and $10,000 per month on Google Ads. Experiment a bit, see what you can afford, and find what works best for the needs of your company.

Develop a PPC Strategy

The first strategy choice you need to make is where you want to run ads. Google offers two primary ad networks. The Google Search Network targets active searchers, people on a mission to find something, whereas the Google Display Network (GDN) places your ads in front of people who are browsing the internet. Naturally, active searchers click on ads and convert more often, but the GDN brings a unique set of benefits. It's an excellent space for gaining brand awareness, and clicks in the GDN are less pricey than those on the Search Network.

Choose the Search Network if your budget is small. You can reach people who are actively in search of what you offer, run ads against the keywords that are most likely to drive conversions, and more easily measure your ROI and justify your efforts. Choose the Display Network if you want to expand your reach beyond the Search Network, retarget existing web visitors, or improve brand awareness.

Then you need to decide what you want to get out of your ads. When I was a CMO, I built my PPC strategy around an understanding of which keywords our prospects used the most. I would drop a Google ad on keywords that we thought were essential but that for whatever reason we did not rank particularly high for. If we weren't in the top three listings on page one for very important keywords, then we would buy an ad. I would also buy ad space on some keywords that performed well for us, including keywords that used our name. For example, before Thycotic merged with Centrify, if someone searched *Thycotic*, the first thing they saw was an ad for Thycotic. That's because our competitors also bought ads on our name, and I didn't want searchers to see those ads before they saw anything from us.

I also used the same tactic as our competitors and dropped ads on their names. The key to doing this is to be intentional about what you want the ad to say. Tailor the ad to the specific keyword that references your competitor, and, as always, make sure that you do so in a way that aligns with your overall messaging. For example, at Thycotic, we used simplicity as our primary differentiator, so I would buy ad space on keywords like [*competitor's name*] *documentation* or [*competitor's name*] *user guide*, which linked to content about how much simpler our products were.

Another good rule of thumb is that if someone searches for competitors (or their products) by name, you can assume that they are a bit further along in the buyer's journey. They might already be a customer of your competitor and already understand the importance of your product. That means that you can drop an ad that uses later-stage content. If someone Googles a competitor's product, drop an ad offering a free trial to your product. When going this route, however, remember that while you can use a competitor's name as a keyword, you cannot reference them in the ad itself, as it violates trademark law.

Keep in mind that for Google Ads, negative keywords (keywords you *don't* want to trigger your ads) are as important as regular keywords. Help your agency understand what they are. They'll figure this out as they perform maintenance, but there's no harm in giving them a head start. For example, you may want your ads to trigger for variations of *executive leadership coaching* but not for *one-to-one executive leadership coaching*. *One-to-one* is your negative keyword.

Collaborating with Search and Ad Experts

I consider my Google agency as an extension of my company. Anything important that I share with the internal marketing team also goes to my Google team. I've heard countless stories of companies that launched a new product but didn't tell their SEO agency until after it was released. Or they updated their website without telling their agency. This can be disastrous. Each Google ad links to a landing page. Sometimes a website update changes the URL of a landing page. If the ad team doesn't know, then that company pays for clicks that go straight to an error page.

Monitoring the cost and outcome of your ad campaigns and measuring results against your advertising goals is as important as running the ads in the first place. I have a monthly meeting with the SEO and PPC staff and agencies to review strategy, specific PPC ads, look at our results, and discuss future content such as white papers and blogs. I also give them any pertinent updates, including those on changes to our positioning, our website, or our products themselves, so that they can change the ads they run and our SEO strategy accordingly.

Finally, remember that using Google Ads is part art, part science. Your agency will test one ad against another, one landing page against another, and then some. Testing is critical to a positive outcome. Test headlines, messages, and the offers. But stay vigilant. If you aren't satisfied with the results after a reasonable amount of time, it is completely fine to look for a contractor or agency that better fits your style of work and helps you reach your goals.

CHAPTER 4

Create a High-Performing Website

In the digital world, a website is equivalent to a store. Actually, more than that—it is a store, if that store were open 24/7, omnipresent, could hold an infinite number of people, and had an army of sales robots. In other words, the website is a modern miracle, and one of the most valuable marketing and sales tools.

The outside world sees every company through its website. The website communicates everything about its company—what it values, how it positions itself, how it's organized, and what type of culture it cultivates. Does the website present a rosy, cheery view of the world? Or are its theme and colors dark and imposing? A lot of people say that a company is the people in it, and I agree. But in the B2B world, the website represents the people. As a CMO, I considered the website my responsibility. I took pride in it. When colleagues or friends or anybody went to our website, I wanted them to see a sparkling representation of our company.

Because I viewed the website as a reflection of me and my team, I dedicated a significant amount of time to it. And high-performing websites take a lot of time. They aren't events. They are processes of constant testing and improvement.

In Thycotic's early days, every single person worked in a cubicle. I had the same size cubicle as everyone else on my marketing team. I made sure that the person with the cubicle closest to mine was our webmaster, an incredible talent by the name of Josh Frankel. If I heard a conversation going on about the website, I could drop in, listen, and offer my perspective. If I had an idea or something that I wanted to bounce off him, I would just bring it up right away. Josh might not have loved this setup—he always worked with earbuds in—but he and I shared a passion for delivering a high-performing website.

As Thycotic, and our offices, became bigger and we all became busier, I couldn't maintain quite the same level of connection. But I got as close to that ideal as I could. I've noticed that some CMOs don't recognize the full importance of their websites and instead treat them as glorified billboards. And even if they understand the significance, they don't always understand what a high-performing website is and how to diagnose problems that prevent their websites from performing at a high level. They spend much of their time thinking about aesthetics. While those matter, they're the more superficial aspects of a website. And, frankly, a competent web designer can handle those on their own.

The most important aspect of a website is whether it performs. For all the enigmatic and artistic aspects of website design, at the end of the day it's like anything else in business. Metrics reveal performance, and you must rely on facts to guide decision-making. That's what we did at Thycotic. I evaluated my website through the lens of several key performance indicators (KPIs), which revealed its overall health. In this chapter, I will lay out what those metrics are, why they matter, and how to improve them. Here is a simple summary chart to help you gauge how well your website is performing:

Website KPIs	Poor	Good	Great
Overall Traffic	Varies based on several factors such as business size	Varies	Varies
Traffic Growth Month over Month	<5%	5–10%	>10% and up
Conversion Rate	<4%	4–6%	6% and up
Bounce Rate	>60%	40–60%	<40%
Session Duration	<2.5 min	2.5–4 min	>4 min
Page Load Time	>2 sec	1–2 sec	<1 sec
Page Size	>2 MB	1–2 MB	<1 MB
New vs. Returning Visitors	<20% new (varies based on several factors)	20–40% new	>40% new
Pages Per Visit	<2	2–4	4 and up

I've broken these KPIs down into categories: the primary KPIs, which make the biggest impact on success, and the secondary KPIs, which impact performance of the primary KPIs. We will start with the primary KPIs and the ways to improve them. Then we will look at the secondary KPIs, examine how they impact the primary ones, and ways to improve those as well.

At the end of the day, a high-performing website must contribute to revenue. It does that by doing two things: consistently increasing the number of people who visit and interact with the website, and then converting a high percentage of those visitors into leads. Therefore, the three primary KPIs to track are overall traffic, growth of traffic month to month, and visitor-to-lead conversion rate.

Overall Traffic

Overall traffic refers to the total number of web users who visit a website. It's a common way to measure a business's effectiveness at attracting an audience.

- **Good performance:** Varies based on several factors such as business size and maturity, though the more website visitors, the better.
- **How to measure it:** Google Analytics, Semrush, Alexa, Crazy Egg, the dashboard on your content management system (CMS).
- **How to improve it:** Ultimately, digital ad campaigns and other related marketing tactics bring visitors in. I'll go into far more detail about great campaigns later in the book, and I have already covered some of the best ways to increase web traffic, such as organic searches and PPCs. There are three basic things you can do to attract visitors: email newsletters, guest blogging, and engage in online communities.

Email Newsletters

Once you build a subscriber list, a newsletter is a great, inexpensive way to drive traffic to your site and keep subscribers interested in and up to date on your company. When setting a newsletter cadence, be careful not to overwhelm subscribers. If you send out announcements, general advertising emails, promotions, and offers on a regular basis, don't send a newsletter every week. Consider sending a newsletter every two weeks or once a month.

The content of your newsletter then becomes the key to success. At Thycotic, we designed each newsletter around a simple on-brand, easily recognizable theme. Then we applied it to our template. While there are infinite forms that a newsletter might take, Josh, my webmaster at Thycotic, developed a template that I believe worked best. At the top, in a section called

What's New and Trending, we put the latest news that related to that week's theme. Next, we had a Featured Content section that included a snippet from (and links to) something we had developed that we were proud of and thought would resonate with customers.

We closed with an anchor, a personalized section where we would input the recipient's name. For example, for someone named Dave, we called it Dave's Cybersecurity News. Here, we linked to bread-and-butter pieces of content that we knew would connect with our list, even if the first two shiny and new items didn't. Somewhere in there—it would change depending on the content—we always included a call to action. Something that got the newsletter readers to the web page to download content, a free trial, or to schedule a demo. We kept this on theme and tailored to the content of the newsletter.

Guest Blogging

Blogging for someone else's website or having a recognized expert blog for you promotes your site and establishes authority. It can be tricky to find good guest bloggers, and it's impossible if they don't receive some compensation. Be ready to either pay the guest bloggers or do something for them such as write a blog or appear on a podcast. The best run, most successful blogs have high profiles. The bloggers typically are busy people and have to invest their time wisely.

At Thycotic, we first approached any high-profile cybersecurity writers we had a relationship with. As your network grows, you will naturally build these sorts of relationships, and you can reach out to these people to ask if they would like to write for your blog. After we tapped our existing network, we expanded our search. I've found that experts like talking to other experts much more than speaking to a marketing intern tasked with cold-calling on LinkedIn. So our subject matter experts and high-profile employees reached out to leading industry bloggers. This approach worked and as an added bonus led to new personal relationships with industry leaders.

Engage in Online Communities

We live in the age of crowdsourcing. People read reviews from sites such as Yelp before they go to a restaurant or beauty salon, and they scour verified buyer reviews before they order anything online. On top of all that, people increasingly bounce purchasing decisions off their online peer groups in forums like Facebook, Reddit, and Discord. Many people, especially those of Generation Z, trust what they read on these pages. Nobody ever says something nice on Reddit or Discord unless they mean it. The anonymity allows an aggressive candor.

These online communities serve as a great source of information for buyers, and in my experience they generate high-quality leads. People who go to a message board for a particular issue or product usually really care about that topic. You don't see many loiterers in the cybersecurity subreddit. The key is to have a consistent presence in these communities.

When I worked for Thycotic, we used a tool to track posts on each of the primary online forums. Whenever someone posted about one of our areas of expertise, someone from our company responded. Some companies give away key chains or other tchotchkes like that. But almost nobody wants those things. We were always extra careful never to come across as sales-y in our posts. We knew we would get crushed if it seemed like we just dropped in to peddle our wares. Instead, we reached out like any member of a community, techie to techie, and tried to be as helpful as possible. If applicable, or if we had some blog posts that went into detail about whatever challenge the poster had, we would drop a link to the content on our website.

Monitoring and responding to all of these posts takes a lot of extra time and effort. But it pays off. One post with a link back to our website will stay up for years and generate potential leads for years. This also helped us build trust. All of the security professionals who moved through that thread would see us and our expertise. Then when they ended up in the market for a new PAM solution, they would call us first. I, as the CMO, even kept my own tool that tracked the posts on many of these sites. Whenever I saw one that we hadn't responded to, I notified the person who handled the responses.

I didn't do this to micromanage or jump down my employee's throat. It was just me helping her out, and I trusted her to do the rest. I strove to stay involved in the process and model the sort of detail-oriented behavior I expected. To me, the difference between an A performance and a B performance always rests in the little details. Yet I knew that I couldn't just sit on a mountaintop dispensing dicta. People wouldn't buy it. I had to be willing to get into the nitty-gritty just like everyone else.

Another great way to stay involved in communities across all social media platforms is to cultivate them. For example, while at Thycotic, I created a cybersecurity professional group on LinkedIn. I wanted to use it as a forum. We rarely referenced Thycotic in our posts. Instead we shared information, articles related to the industry, and encouraged everyone else to do the same. I ended up retiring before the full plan came to fruition, but the endgame was to use this group as a database that would help us build thought leadership and grow revenue. I would have thousands of ideal target buyers gathered in one place, which essentially would be a list of names I could target with ads in their LinkedIn feeds.

Traffic Growth Month over Month (MoM)

Traffic Growth Month over Month refers to the monthly growth in website visits, sometimes called "sessions."

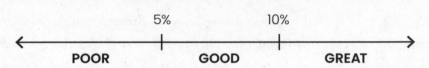

Why it's important: Continually growing traffic quickly has a major impact on the bottom line. For example, a company that brings in one hundred thousand leads in one month and has a 10 percent rate of growth would bring in ten thousand more visitors the next month, then about eleven thousand the month after, and so on. With a 5 percent visitor-to-lead conversion rate, ten thousand visitors become two hundred more leads. With each lead assigned a $100 value, that's $20,000 more in potential revenue after just one month.

Good performance: 10 percent.

How to measure it: Google Analytics, Semrush, Alexa, Crazy Egg, the dashboard on your CM.

How to improve it: Many of the strategies that drive overall traffic to your website are discussed in this book. But, for whatever reasons, if growth stagnates, there are three tactics I've used to get going again: repurpose content, establish content pillars, and deploy promotions or contests.

Repurpose Content

Repurposing content that has delivered good results in the past can help you reach new audiences on different mediums. It gives you much more bang for your buck. Blog posts can become downloadable guides; webinars can become videos.

Establish Content Pillars

Search engines try to direct searchers to the most credible sources, so they promote websites with encyclopedic knowledge bases and any content that dives deep into the details. At Thycotic, we created pages that went in-depth about what PAM is, defined various terms, and gave histories of cybersecurity. I call these content pillars because they support the rest of the website. On their own, they don't convert a lot of visitors into leads, but they draw in a lot of visitors and can be stuffed full of links to higher-converting pages.

Deploy Promotions or Contests

Contests and other promotions can provide a huge short-term boost to traffic, which often translates to sustained growth. Each year around the holiday season, Thycotic ran the 12 Days of Thycotic promotion. Anyone who came to the web page would get one free prize a day. This type of promotion can offer small things like T-shirts, mugs, or hats or larger prizes like discounts or free access to events.

During my last few years at Thycotic, this campaign blew up. Each December, we saw an absurd 35 percent increase in web traffic. It got so popular that my webmaster had to remove our December stats from quarterly trend reporting because we performed so well in that month that it skewed everything else. The success of this campaign came, in part, from the quality of the prizes we offered. Before we offered something as a giveaway, we went through several drafts of the design and had the people around the office try it out. We would only offer something that we ourselves wanted. Some companies give away key chains or other tchotchkes like that. But almost nobody wants those things. They're clutter and do nothing to get people to respond.

The other big factor for promotion success is timing. People often get in the holiday mood and tend to work less in the middle of December. They have the time to remember to come back to the same website every day to get their prizes. Try to pick a date for your promotion when people have time to notice. The holidays work great, as does late summer.

Conversion Rate

Conversation rate shows the percentage of website visitors that takes a desired action on your website. This action converts them from visitors to leads (or customers). The desired action might be downloading a white paper, signing up for a free trial, or completing a purchase.

CONVERSION RATE

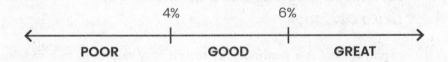

Why it's important: The entire purpose of a website is to convert visitors to leads. This is, in some ways, the single most important metric because it tracks the percentage of web page visitors that become leads. A high conversion rate will fuel tremendous revenue growth. The table below shows the extent to which small changes in website visitor-to-lead conversion rate (CVR) impact revenue. In this example, the visitors stay steady at one hundred thousand, and we assume each lead is worth $100. The difference between the top and bottom range is nearly $500,000 in revenue a month.

Visitors/Month	CVR	Leads	Revenue ($100/lead)
100,000	2%	2,000	$200,000
100,000	5%	5,000	$500,000
100,000	7%	7,000	$700,000

Good performance: 4–6 percent.

How to measure it: Google Analytics, Semrush, Hotjar, VWO, Google Optimize, Optimizely.

How to improve it: A high CVR relies on nearly everyone on the marketing team. It requires you to bring in the right visitors to your website and provide them with the right content. From a website perspective, there are two main ways to improve CVR: conduct split testing and reduce friction.

Conduct Split Testing: Act Like a Scientist, Think Like a Designer

A/B, or split, testing is a methodology to test how variations to a website impact user behavior. It more or less follows the scientific method: if we take *X* action, we will achieve *Y* result due to *Z*. Then you run a test and analyze the data. In this context, you want to see the impact of changes to a web page on the CVR.

Many organizations run these sorts of tests but rarely in a way that moves the needle. In my experience, this is because they attempt to test everything they can and design experiments to see whether a blue Download Now button converts more frequently than a green one. They might see a slight shift of less than 1 percent in the CVR. This doesn't really tell them anything.

Instead of focusing on such nitpicky tests, we at Thycotic focused on testing more substantial changes to a web page like adding or removing a video, or changing how we describe our value proposition. I would rather have a test show me a 25 percent drop in our CVR than a 1 percent improvement because that tells me much more about what our audiences want. We took those insights into what resonated with our customers and applied them to each part of the marketing process, including other parts of the website, our email campaigns, and our web ad design. A/B testing on the web page became a reactor core that powered the rest of our operation. In my experience, there are four main actions you can test: edit, add, subtract, and reposition.

Edit

When people think about split testing, they usually think about edit tests, where you change the content to see what resonates the most with buyers. For example, you might want to see if a new value proposition, messaging and positioning angle, customer pain point, logo, or rebrand will move the needle. It's best to test those changes on a few web pages first. If the change substantially decreases the test pages' performance, then I'd recommend reconsidering the changes before you roll them out. If, on the other hand, the change improves CVR, then it serves as an excellent proof of concept.

We once ran an extremely successful editing test that proved an important point: unusual or surprising web pages usually convert at a much higher rate. Early in the development stage for the Thycotic website, we used a lot of stock photography on our "Customers" page. Stock photos are like wallpaper—they just blend into the background. Yet most companies still use them because they are cheaper and faster than alternatives.

Our website manager, Josh, looked at the "Customers" page and realized that the stock photos of smiling twenty-something models in tailored suites looked nothing like our customers. We sold cybersecurity software to IT professionals. So Josh went through the file of our customers' headshots and found the people who looked like our typical IT professionals, with their glasses, signs of age, and somewhat awkward smiles. We featured their photos on the page, and the CVR jumped. Suddenly, instead of drab pedestrian photos of people shaking hands in sleek offices, visitors saw a group of people in whom they could recognize themselves. It made a real impact on our potential customers.

Add

Test the impact on CVR by adding something to the web page. The most common additions are headlines, logos of the high-profile companies that you service (which builds credibility), graphics, charts, and videos. There are many possibilities of how you might display the same information. Does a graph work better than long blocks of text to display your product features? Does a video with somebody clicking through the product work better than a brochure-like section? Does a combination of the two work better? Are there certain pieces of information that when added to a page, boosts CVRs?

Subtract

Because there are many ways to display information, a lot of companies fall into the trap of stuffing their pages with too much content. Anything you might add and test, you can take away and test. Does this page really need a video, several graphics, and a full blog post? Do people respond well to videos, or would they rather read and skim the information at their own pace? Is there some content on this page that is unrelated to what the page is about? Unnecessary pieces of content dampen CVRs. When people read content that they didn't look for, they get annoyed and leave before they convert. Try running tests where you stick to the bare essentials for each page.

Reposition

In these tests, you keep all the same content on the page but just reposition it. This usually leads to what you might call no-duh realizations. For example, we ran a test on a Thycotic product page where we moved a video from the top to the bottom and moved the information about the product features and the free trial to the top. Conversion spiked! People had gone to the page explicitly looking for the free trial, and we made it easier to find. It also created a less intuitive result: our product-related video plays didn't drop. This proves an important point—people stay on a website and web page when they get what they want. When the video came first, visitors stopped scrolling and left after the video. With the free trial first, they downloaded the trial, which converted into a lead, and then because they were curious, they watched the video.

Design Tests Based off User Patterns

A great way to find new needle-moving tests is to design them based on how customers behave when they visit your site. At Thycotic, we did this with a tool called heat mapping. Heat mapping shows you the website in infrared, predator-style vision. But it's not Arnold Schwarzenegger scanning for life; it's a representation of where people spend their time. It shows you, in aggregate, how far down each page most people scroll and where their cursor rests. The longer visitors hover over something, the redder it becomes. If they never interact with a part of a page, it will show up green or blue.

Remember, the goal of a website is to have 100 percent of what someone is looking for. Nothing more, nothing less. Heat mapping can help you get closer to that goal. If there are, for example, images, tools, videos, or blocks of text, that most people don't interact with at all, then you can use that information to try something new. Does a different call to action acquire more heat and conversions? Does simply deleting the cold spots impact the page CVR? If you apply some of the hot features from one page to another, what happens?

As an added bonus, using this sort of activity tracking also helps you refine website content. You'll know what videos get the most play, which graphics work, and what sort of articles people like the most. You'll start to understand how your audience likes to be spoken to. Once you know that, you can incorporate that knowledge into the content production process. It all becomes a big cycle, where you use the metrics from your website to help improve your content strategy.

Reduce Friction

In most cases, a customer converts by filling out a form. Visitors are less likely to fill out longer forms. Make sure to capture exactly and only the data that the sales team needs to effectively follow up. Focus on making the form as simple to fill out as possible, such as using drop-down menus for location and job title.

The second thing to examine for friction are your calls to action sitewide. A web page with several confusing calls to action will bounce a prospect more often than it will convert one. Make sure each page has a goal and includes a call to action relevant to that goal. Test different calls to action with different pages to make sure you maximize the CVR. The way you display that call to action matters, too. Buttons and forms should always use descriptive, active text. For example, "Submit" won't perform as well as "Download Now," and "Get Now" will probably outperform both.

Finally, a good, easy way to improve CVR is to add catchall calls to action to the bottom of any page that doesn't already have one. People often land on a page and quickly scroll through it to see if it is what they want. If it's not, they leave the page when they reach the bottom. If you have a call to action at the bottom, something like, "Learn more about [topic of web page]," that person might convert instead of merely leave.

Secondary KPIs

The three KPIs previously covered give the clearest sense of a website's health. If your website is in the good-to-great range of all those KPIs, then you're doing great. If, however, performance is lagging, and you've tried all the improvement but can't turn it around, you might need to dig deeper. Underperformance in any of these six secondary KPIs will negatively impact either the traffic numbers, CVR, or both. The secondary KPIs are bounce rate and session duration, page load time, page size, new vs. returning visitors, and pages per visit.

Bounce Rate and Session Duration

These two metrics are so interconnected that it's impossible to talk about one without talking about the other. Any measure taken to improve one will also improve the other. We will start with bounce rate.

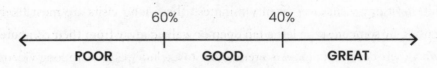

BOUNCE RATE

60%   40%

POOR   GOOD   GREAT

Why it's important: A bounce is when a visitor hits a single page on a site and then leaves. Successful websites are sticky, meaning they make visitors hang around and find more useful content as they go through more pages.

This metric impacts the overall conversion rate. Visitors become leads only if they stick around long enough to put in their information. Everybody who bounces is a missed opportunity. Google also notices and punishes high bounce rates. It ranks pages with higher bounce rates lower in the SERPs and charges more for ads that link to them.

Good performance: 40–60 percent.

How to measure it: Google Analytics, Semrush, Alexa, Crazy Egg, the dashboard on your CMS.

SESSION DURATION (min)

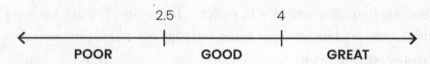

Good performance: 2.5–4 minutes

Why it's important: Session duration measures how long each visitor spends on a site. The longer the visit, the more meaningful the interaction between the prospect and the brand, and the more likely the visitor is to convert.

How to measure it: Google Analytics, Semrush, Hotjar. Make sure to always filter out any visits over twenty minutes. These long visits are most likely caused by someone who left a tab open or walked away from their computer with their browser open. Also remember to exclude pages with long videos, webinars, or other playable content, as they skew session duration.

How to improve both: A high bounce rate and low session duration reveals that the content doesn't deliver what the website promised it would. There are two things you can do to prevent this: quickly give visitors the content they want and, audit the full website.

Quickly Give Visitors the Content They Want

Somewhere along the line, somebody thought that the best way to get customers' attention online was to blast them with as much information as possible. This, I assume, must have been the reasoning behind things like pop-up ads and auto-play videos. The same reasoning dominated the old model of marketing such as TV and radio advertising. Namely that the only way to get someone's attention is to interrupt something they actually want to see.

This line of thinking was nonsense then, and it's ridiculous now. Nobody wants a pop-up ad or a video that auto plays, even if the pop-up or video are directly related to what they searched for. Few things bounce a visitor from a website faster. Prospects want the content that they clicked on and nothing else. Not the video, and never, ever, ever the pop-up ad.

Audit the Full Website

About every six weeks, I blocked out a few hours to review every single page of the Thycotic website. I had talented, dedicated people working hard on the website, so I didn't want to micromanage them. But as the CMO, I needed to look for anything that had slipped through the cracks, and I always found something.

In my audit, I would look for all the common website bouncers: dated content, misleading headlines, broken links, unintuitive navigation, and cluttered and unappealing presentations. I also looked for blocks of text that were too long and made sure that we broke them up with headers, graphics, or images.

Page Load Time

Page load time is the average amount of time it takes for a web page to show up on your screen.

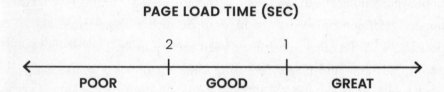

PAGE LOAD TIME (SEC)

Why it's important: Website conversion rates drop by an average of 4.42 percent with each additional second of load time. Most visitors expect a site to load in under three seconds, and if doesn't, they just leave. Even if they stick around, the long load time distracts from the content, frustrates the prospect, and erodes their trust in the company. This is another area where the webmaster impacts SEO, as slow loading sites rank lower in search results.

Good performance: 1–2 seconds.

How to measure it: Google Analytics, Semrush, Alexa, Crazy Egg, the dashboard on your CMS.

How to improve it: This is the sort of thing that a webmaster must stay on top of. The best way to reduce load time is through a cocktail of programming solutions and third-party products, all of which require some level of technical skill. I won't go into too much detail here, but a few of the elements that make the biggest difference are to use a content delivery network, enable caching, use lazy load, and evaluate your hosting provider.

Use a Content Delivery Network (CDN)

A CDN is a localized network for delivery of your website and allows for a fast, regionalized delivery of your web assets.

- **Enable caching:** Caching is when a server, browser, or CDN temporarily stores files so they don't all have to reload each time a prospect visits a page. This makes a significant difference, though it only reduces load time for returning prospects.
- **Use lazy load:** Lazy load prevents images from loading until a visitor scrolls to it. Images are usually the largest file size of anything on the site, and loading them one at a time greatly decreases overall load times.
- **Evaluate your hosting provider:** If you see long load times even after you've made other tweaks, chances are that your hosting platform is to blame. I recommend exploring other options until you find one that delivers a faster load time.

Page Size

Page size refers to the downloaded file size of a given web page.

PAGE SIZE (MB)

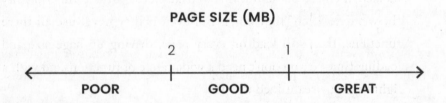

Why it's important: Load time alone does not give the clearest idea of a user experience. Often, when you measure load time, you do it on your own CDN, and with ideal circumstances. A huge page might load quickly there, but very slowly on someone else's computer, and it may be impossible to access from mobile. To ensure a uniformly positive experience and consistently low load times, reduce page size as much as possible. This also helps with SEO rankings, as Google prefers smaller pages.

Good performance: 1 MB or less.

How to measure it: Google Analytics, Semrush, Alexa, Crazy Egg, the dashboard on your CMS.

How to improve it: This is another metric that relies heavily on the webmaster. Usually, a combination of coding and design work affects page size. The low-hanging fruit techniques that I recommend are to compress images, switch themes, and reduce plug-ins and modules.

- **Compress images:** Images can have metadata, such as location and camera type, and other artifacts embedded in their file. Image compression can remove that, reducing the file size by up to 60 percent without changing the visual quality.
- **Switch themes:** If all of your pages are massive, you might need to consider switching themes. A lot of companies sell heavy-duty, bloated themes. Sometimes, a website needs all the functionality these offer. Often, they don't. But even if they never use all these functions, they still load on every page, driving up page size and loading time. If you don't need a wide range of functions, go with a lightweight, streamlined theme.
- **Reduce plug-ins and modules:** Plug-ins and modules add significant size to every page. Some of them, like a web chat function, help a lot. Keep those. But I would strike any module that doesn't directly improve CVR.

New vs. Returning Visitors

New visitors are people who are coming to your site for the first time on a device. Returning visitors have visited your site previously.

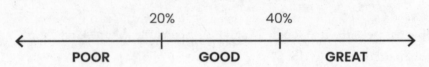

% NEW VISITORS

Why it's important: To survive, a company needs a healthy mix of new and returning traffic. Obviously, new traffic is great, but prospects rarely convert to leads the first time on a site, and in the B2B world they almost never buy the first time they visit a site. If you have a small proportion of returning visitors, chances are you also have a low conversion rate. New businesses are an exception because they grow rapidly, so they might see new visitors in the 90 percent range.

Good performance: About 30 percent new visitors (depends on factors like business maturity).

How to measure it: Google Analytics, Semrush, the dashboard on your CMS.

How to improve it: A lot of the campaigns and tactics that we discussed to drive overall traffic also helps lure people back. If you notice plenty of new traffic but no return customers, I'd recommend that you publish content more frequently, create a community or loyalty program, or invest in remarketing campaigns.

- **Publish content more frequently:** People don't come back to a site that stays stagnant. Why should they? What's new for them to learn? Regularly publishing quality content, and then advertising that in a newsletter, on social media, or through PPC ads, gives them a reason to come back.

- **Create a community or loyalty program:** Build a club for your customers and evangelists. This can be a forum on your site (or on any platform), or a special rewards program available to customers and repeat visitors.

- **Invest in remarketing campaigns:** Remarketing is when you buy ads to target someone who has, in some way, interacted with your brand. If somebody visited the Thycotic website and never came back, we would capture their IP address and then hound them with ads. YouTube ads, Facebook ads, LinkedIn ads, really anything we could use to try to get them to visit. We did set a time limit on this—if someone didn't come back within thirty days, they probably wouldn't come back at all.

Pages per Visit

Pages per visit is a measure of how many web pages a user views on a single visit to a website.

PAGES PER VISIT

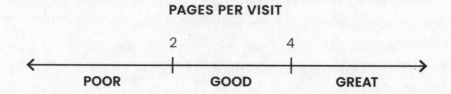

Why it's important: Pages per visit is the average number of pages a prospect views in a single session. This metric gauges visitors' interest and engagement with the site. The more pages they go to, the more they connect to the content, and the more likely they are to convert. There is, however, a sweet spot in pages per visit. Too many pages per visit could indicate the visitor couldn't find what they were looking for, or didn't have enough opportunities to convert to a lead.

Good performance: Two to four pages per visit. On a practical level, someone who hits a landing page and immediately converts will then go to a thank-you page. This counts as two pages per visit. The lowest number of pages it takes to convert is two. If they click through to four or more pages without converting, they're not ready to convert or they can't find what they need.

How to measure it: Google Analytics, Semrush, the dashboard on your CMS. Key ways to increase pages per visit include adding bread crumb navigation and incorporating cross links.

Add Bread Crumb Navigation

Each website has levels. Think of the home page as level zero. Then any pages that deal with a broad category like products or the company history are level-one pages. Each page that deals with a more specific topic is another level. So, for example, a specific product page might be a level two page, while a product feature page would be level three.

When visitors first reach a web page, they're often coming from a Google search that led them to a level three or four page. Our research at Thycotic showed that most people enter in a lower level and click back a few levels to learn more about the company in a broad sense before going deeper into the details. If they can't easily navigate the site, they often bounce. Creating bread crumb navigation—often in the form of a drop-down menu—can help facilitate that movement through the site.

Another important note here is that on your home page, your bread crumb navigation should link to the sections of your site that generate the most traffic and the most leads. Some companies think that if they have a page, they should have a link for it on the home page. Those menu headers are prime real estate—don't waste it. This, of course, can get more difficult if office politics gets involved. It's not uncommon for someone with a C-level position to try to get their department on the top banner of the website menu, even if their pages only generate 1 percent of the traffic to the site. The CMO and webmaster should always be able to explain exactly why they've given the best spaces to the links they have.

Add Cross Links

To get people to visit more pages, make it easier for them to jump around from page to page. This is a process called cross linking, where you essentially create a network of links. I like to think of a website as a city. There are highways that lead to the city and ramps to get from the highway to the city. In the digital world, the ramps are any avenue that leads people to a website, such as Google searches, PPC ads, in-person referrals, social media posts, and emails.

Once inside the city, there are all sorts of streets, large and small, that help people get around. Those are crosslinks. And, ultimately, in most cities, all major roads lead to the very heart. The crosslink infrastructure should be the same in your website. Just keep in mind that the heart of a website isn't the home page; it is the pages that create most conversions.

Obviously, you can't link every single page to one of the high-converting pages on the site. Instead, work on finding crosslink opportunities that make sense. Hyperlink parts of your blog posts to related content and then create related content widgets at the bottom or sides of the page that will offer other articles those visitors might want to read. Likewise, use featured content widgets or banners at the bottom of pages to direct people to high-performing web pages. You can almost think of these as internal ads that draw attention to your best and highest trafficked content.

CHAPTER 5

Implement the Right Marketing Technology Stack

As of 2022, over seven thousand marketing software technologies are available for sale. Combined, they make up a $121 billion market. It's a massive number, enough to make anyone's head spin. From this dizzying array of options, each company can select a series of software they will use, a Martech stack.

A 2021 study by Gartner Group found that on average, companies allocate 26 percent of their marketing budget to their Martech stack, which makes it the largest single marketing expenditure. Yet according to a 2020 Gartner Marketing Technology Survey, marketing leaders leverage only half of their Martech's potential. This represents a huge waste. Most organizations burn money on tools they don't use or fail to get the most out of what they've already bought.

To implement and fully leverage the right Martech stack, you first need to understand its potential. Used properly, Martech enables amazingly sophisticated marketing at scale. It does this through three primary interrelated functions. It makes day-to-day operations easier, allows for the creation of campaigns that target extremely specific audiences at the exact moment they want to buy, and collects, manages, and organizes data, which, in part, makes the first two functions possible.

The twenty-first century economy runs on data. While better data has always afforded businesses a competitive advantage, never before has so much and such diverse data been available. The titanic companies of the period—Google, Facebook, Amazon, Apple—all grew as large as they did, in part, because they cornered the data market. Similarly, HVDM relies on expert data management to generate results. It requires constant monitoring of metrics to best understand which strategies work best and which don't. But more important than that, it relies on consumer data.

The velocity comes from the ability to target the perfect prospect with the perfect ad at the absolute perfect moment. In other words, it requires a comprehensive portrait of prospective buyers combined with an exhaustive catalog of their past actions. This, of course, is a lot of data. The rise of this style of marketing has contributed to humans producing, capturing, and storing data at a completely unprecedented rate. According to Domo, a business intelligence software producer, people created 2.5 quintillion data bytes per day through their internet activity in 2020.

To gain a competitive advantage, you need to leverage data. That requires the right technology. This chapter will help you select or streamline your Martech stack. Let's start with a fundamental rule: let strategy dictate the technology.

Let Strategy Dictate Technology

As we all know, but sometimes forget, technology is not strategy. Technology supports and enables strategy, not the other way around. Before you start building (or updating) your Martech stack, it's crucial to devise your marketing strategy and get executive buy-in. Map out exactly how you plan to reach your target audience. Consider new technology only after you've adopted a strategy and analyzed the alternatives. If you can't implement specific parts of the new strategy, then consider new technology to fill the gap. Far too many executives shortcut this process and buy technology they don't need, which inevitably becomes shelfware.

That being said, expanding Martech capabilities will give you access to new strategies. It will also reveal new opportunities, and new needs, that can be addressed with other technology purchases. The tech stack, much like the strategy it supports, constantly evolves. It becomes a cycle: the strategy requires new technology to improve velocity, the new technology makes higher-velocity strategies possible, which eventually require more technology and create more opportunities for efficiently growing revenue. Because each strategy varies dramatically, it's impossible to give a one-size-fits-all Martech stack.

Any HVDM campaign requires Martech that provides a fundamental set of core capabilities. In this chapter I explain those core capabilities and recommend software in the rare case when a single technological tool is dominant in the field. Then I go through some of the technologies that I consider should-haves for an HVDM strategy. Finally, I look at the future of the Martech stack and how the next generation of products will create even more velocity. I do not recommend specific products. Instead, I suggest you research different providers to find ones that meet your needs. Just make sure that whatever tools you choose interact seamlessly with one another.

What follows might be a bit overwhelming. Remember, Rome was not built in a day, and neither was Google. You can't rush to implement the Martech stack. Instead, focus on your area of greatest need and build from there. The Martech stack is never finished—it constantly grows and becomes more refined and optimized.

The Foundations of the HVDM Martech Stack: Your Must-Have Tools

HVDM, as I've conceived of it and practiced it, cannot happen without these core technologies: customer relationship management (CRM), marketing automation software, web analytics, content management systems, and ad tech.

Customer Relationship Management

CRM tools store everything about a customer and their entire relationship with a company. How often did they visit the website? How many calls have they had with the sales team? What content did they download? What company are they from? What stage of the buyer's journey are they in? What stage of the sales process?

Sales teams rely on CRM—it stores all the information that will inform their next actions and how they follow up with leads. Executives and the marketing team use it to track revenue, monitor how prospects move through the pipeline, and assess individual salespeople's performance.

CRM bridges the gap between marketing and sales teams. In B2B companies, marketers lose control once they hand a lead to sales. But they rely on sales to meet their revenue goals, so marketers need a way to make sure that the sales team delivers. CRM software provides that. With it, marketers can understand whether or not the sales team executed their agreed upon processes.

Marketing Automation Software

Marketing automation software automatically sends personalized messages to prospects through such avenues as emails and social media channels. It works with a set of rules. For example, when a prospect watches a webinar, the software knows to send them emails related to that software. This reduces manual labor, freeing up employees to spend more time strategizing and completing other duties. I recommend buying your CRM and marketing automation software as a package because one relies on the other.

Web Analytics

Web analytics software tracks, measures, and reports on website activity, including site traffic, visitor source, and user clicks. This provides deep insight into buyer personas and reveals what works and what doesn't.

Content Management Systems

In HVDM, you must publish content regularly, and to do that, you need a CMS, which provides everything a programming novice needs to create and manage a website. It includes website authoring, collaboration, and administration tools that assist with every type of content, including text, images, videos, and audio. Many come with SEO functionalities that make it easier to optimize content for organic searches. Remember to find a CMS tool that can integrate with your current website infrastructure.

Ad Tech (Google Ads)

While organic traffic often drives most revenue, Google ads play a critical role. They help your company rank for important, competitive keywords and target ideal customers with precision. Due to Google's dominance, Google's search, video, and display ads are still the fastest way to drive visitors to your site. Google Ads is the best tool to use to place those ads.

Extension Technologies: Your Should-Have Tools

There are six technologies that I wouldn't consider core capabilities but that might be necessary depending on your strategy or business model. They are account-based marketing (ABM) tools, sales engagement, social media management, customer intelligence, lead-scoring management software, and conversion rate optimization (CRO).

ABM Tools

We cover ABM in chapter nine. For now, all you need to know is that ABM uses the coordinated efforts of both marketing and sales to target high-value accounts. ABM tools facilitate that by looking for surge signals, or behaviors that indicate a company might want to buy the product. For example, the tool will notify you when several people from the same company search for your product, or when a company lists an available job for the team that would use your solution. It even notifies you when someone searches competitors' websites. Then these tools help you design and buy ads that land directly in front of those people.

While these tools are designed for ABM, they also provide value for HVDM campaigns. They can work with marketing automation software to send leads to sales with more precision and speed. For instance, somebody downloads a white paper. On its own, that isn't enough to send them to sales. But if they download a white paper and the ABM software notices five other people from the same company are Googling your software solution, that tells you that this is a high-quality lead. The lead goes straight to sales based on the behavior of the whole company, not just the one prospect who downloaded the white paper.

Sales Engagement

These tools are best for teams that are serious about sales and marketing alignment. They essentially sit on top of the CRM software and provide a more intuitive platform to interact with leads, trigger activities, log data, and set up meetings. They track sales reps' interactions with prospects and customers and recommend next steps. They also create easy-to-read dashboards to help make sure that no lead slips through the cracks.

Social Media Management

These tools allow you to schedule posts at optimal times, streamline your publishing workflows, and turn social data into meaningful insights. All of this is geared toward optimizing social media strategy and connecting with your audience.

Customer Intelligence

This covers a wide range of tools, all designed to harvest customer opinions about a brand. Any company that makes ads that quickly respond to an incident or a sudden social media trend likely uses some form of this type of software. Some scan the web, especially social media and review aggregating websites, for any brand mentions. They also can scan for internet trends that might relate to your company. For example, if there is a hashtag about cybersecurity software trends, customer intelligence tools can be set up to notify you. This keeps you on top of the conversation about your company and is especially important because people increasingly make decisions based on what they hear about a company. If your brand, for example, gets criticism from anywhere online, you will be alerted to this and be able to respond quickly.

Lead-Scoring Management Software

There is little point in generating huge numbers of lower-quality leads that are not sales ready. In fact, doing so kills sales reps' productivity because they waste time with prospects who are unlikely to ever become customers. Sales and marketing teams determine if a lead is worthy of being passed to sales reps through a process called lead scoring (more on this in chapter six), which runs the calculations that gauge lead quality.

These tools can also add new information to a lead so that you don't have to get everything from your online forms. For example, most sellers want to know the number of people a company employs. Instead of adding a company size line to the online form, your lead management software will find the size of the prospect's company and enter it into the CRM database. The software can also discover the size of specific teams at companies, their tech stack, tools that a company uses, and much more.

CVR Optimization

CRO tools capture data about website visitors. These are the heatmapping and A/B testing tools. There are also specific tools that you can use to create and split test highly personalized landing pages. For example, if someone with an AT&T IP address visits your site, you can create a page that acknowledges where they work and contains all the content that deals with why your product is best for telecommunications providers.

The Data Stack: The Future of Martech

Every company says they want to make data-driven decisions. They want to be smart. Yet as of this writing, nobody can fully leverage the possibilities that data offers. Think about it—the world produces 2.5 quintillion data bytes a day, several orders of magnitude greater than anything humans can perceive. Any individual bit of that data might offer a profound advantage to a company.

Still, even the most sophisticated companies use only a tiny fraction of the data available to them. The vast majority of companies can't even sniff deep data-driven analysis. They might slap a dashboard on top of their CRM and a marketing automation tool and expect to see all their key metrics at a glance. That almost never works. The process to properly extract data from the tools, store, clean it, and turn it into useful graphics and dashboards is incredibly complicated. The real cutting edge of data-driven decision-making goes beyond that. It lies in the ability to process both the company's internal data and the cookie data from across the internet in extreme degrees of detail. Then it uses that detail to deploy far more sophisticated and effective campaigns.

An example of this is multitouch reporting models. At Thycotic, these models use a blend of data from our CRM software and our prospects' cookie data to determine what specific sales or marketing touches make the biggest difference in the sales cycle. The models track and analyze activity for entire accounts, not just individualized buyers. For example, someone from a given company might visit the web page, click through some content, and download a white paper. Then that person's boss comes to your website and downloads a case study followed by an IT person from that company requesting a demo. Then the original person, the one who grabbed the white paper, completes a free trial. Finally, the prospect buys.

An optimized cutting-edge data stack can, first of all, track all of these actions by all of these various individuals. It can also calculate how important each specific touch was to closing the deal. There are different models you can use to attribute this value, but the one we used at Thycotic was a W-shaped attribution model. That model applies the most weight to the very first touch (the white paper) and the very last touch (the free trial).

These have extra weight because they come right before the two major decisions a prospect makes—to become a lead and to become a customer. But these models also track other engagement metrics and see how the interactions between the first and the last touches impact whether a deal closes. For example, the models might show that when people download a particular free tool, they become customers at a much lower rate.

Once you've built the model, you can aggregate and analyze the results. You could, say, look back at the last 600 wins. You might notice that 250 of those wins came from a specific email campaign designed for leads. Or you might notice that once people who have begun to speak to sales personnel download a specific case study, they close much faster than other prospects. You can use this information, and your entire Martech stack, not only to create smarter strategies, but to automate them as well. In the future you will be able to feed these metrics into an AI system that will scan your entire CRM base to find prospects that have started speaking to sales. Then the software will buy ads such as banner ads, PPC ads, and video ads for those prospects that lead them to a personalized landing page with a relevant case study.

A fully optimized data stack combined with new AI capabilities offers endless possibilities. We will probably never be able to utilize every piece of data. But to get as close as you can today, I recommend you use the following core data stack capabilities: extracting, loading, and transforming tools; data storage tools; data cleaning tools; business intelligence dashboards; government compliance; and a data management platform. As with the other technologies, this is not intended to be an exhaustive list but just an overview of the core capabilities needed in the future.

Extracting, Loading, and Transforming Tools

Data accrues in many pieces of software. Before that data can be used, it needs to be extracted and compiled. While this is possible to do manually, the more sophisticated a Martech stack becomes, the less feasible it is to manually extract data. These tools do it for you at regular intervals most commonly once a day, but you can set it to trigger at almost any time frame. Once extracted, that data can be properly analyzed and fed into AI and automation systems that enable faster, smarter advertising.

Data Storage Tools

After extraction, the data needs to go somewhere. The companies that first stored data used to do it on their own servers. But with the exponential growth in the amount of data, that's no longer sustainable. Several companies now sell cloud-based data storage, a cheaper, more scalable option that essentially offers unlimited storage. On top of that, cloud-based data warehouses have much stronger search functions. They can spit out the answer to a query in five seconds, whereas before, it could take up to twenty-five minutes to search a large database. As your marketing operations become more sophisticated, this becomes more important. You might notice a trend, for instance, that companies from a specific region are showing interest in your product, and you want to understand more about it. A high-functioning data warehouse allows you to quickly search for and use all historical data.

Data Cleaning Tools

Data comes into storage dirty. By that I mean the data might contain countless inaccuracies or slight variations. For example, if a website asks for a prospect's employer, one person might input *Google*, one might input *Google Ads*, and a third might input *Alphabet Inc*. These all describe the same company. A well-programmed data cleaner can go through and recognize these inconsistent inputs and combine them so they all show up as Google in a report. These errors have real impacts on closing deals. For instance, one person from Google downloading one white paper would likely not justify sales follow-up. Three people, however, all from Google, all downloading a different content, would justify that sort of follow-up. Clean data allows you to take the best actions as soon as possible.

Business Intelligence Dashboards

Finally, after all the harvesting, extracting, integrating, cleaning, and grouping, you can create visualization tools. Business intelligence software allows you to create dashboards, graphs, and charts that track all of the data collected by a Martech stack. My agency, Integrous Marketing, built me powerful dashboards and graphics that update daily. I could see complex sets of data in simple, actionable reports, and track every dollar spent and each dollar that was brought in. With this, I could easily make new strategy decisions, see how we performed in relation to our goals, and make any adjustments necessary to make sure we hit our targets.

Government Compliance

A database includes a lot of private and personal information, so handling large amounts of data comes with great responsibility and is heavily regulated by the government. There are several tools to make sure that the data stays safe, and your company stays compliant.

Data Management Platform

A data management platform essentially allows you to build hyper-specific, full-blown profiles of almost anybody who encounters your system. It takes as much data as it can get, including purchase history, IP address, physical location, location data, job title, and interactions with the brand. It then compiles this data so a marketer can look at the profile, see exactly who each person is, what they do, and if they seem to want to buy. Then the marketer can build incredibly targeted campaigns designed to hit the most likely buyers.

Get the Most Out of Your Martech Stack and Data Stack

While the right technology goes a long way toward marketing success, it's ultimately the people using the software that maximizes its potential. In my experience, there are two keys to getting the most out of a Martech and data stack: maintain data integrity and invest in the people using the Martech.

Maintain Data Integrity

To be useful, data must move through a system without becoming corrupted or compromised. I call this data integrity, and I like to think of it the way police officers think about evidence. When they collect evidence at a crime scene, police have a strict process that they follow—they tag it, record it, and pass it along through a chain of forensic scientists, clerks, lawyers, and detectives. Specific procedures govern the handling and transfer of evidence at each point in the chain, and all the handoffs are meticulously documented. I do the same with consumer data. A lot of companies I've consulted for don't understand exactly where the data handoff occurs between the sales and marketing teams. This leads to data getting stuck or corrupted. Great leads might slip through the cracks, and the business leaders end up making decisions on incomplete data.

More importantly, lax data integrity creates opportunities for hackers. The most sophisticated HVDM strategies use and store a staggering amount of personal and private data, including credit card information. A private consumer data breach can devastate lives and businesses.

To maintain data integrity, fully audit the flow of data through the company. Map the handoffs, and only give people access to the data they need. Look for any weak spots in your technology infrastructure and patch them to prevent attacks. Make sure everybody knows their responsibilities and that the Martech stack is integrated so none of the data gets stuck in one technology silo.

Invest in the People Using the Martech

Just as a Martech doesn't magically become strategy, it doesn't magically get used correctly, either. My colleagues who own digital marketing agencies constantly hear the same old story from new clients: we just spent tons of money on this hot new technology, and it doesn't work. We have a yearlong subscription, but it slows down our processes more than anything else. More often than not, this happens because the customer expected the new technology to miraculously solve all of their problems. They think that they can just buy the technology, set it up, and let it roll.

That never works. All the technologies above are tools. And tools are only as good as the people who use them. A hammer didn't carve *David*, Michelangelo did. For an investment into any of these technologies to pay off, it's not enough to merely buy the tech. Instead, it needs to be a full-blown commitment. For this reason, I don't purchase any technology unless I'm completely ready to invest the time and resources necessary to integrate it into my operations and fully train users. The stakes are high. According to a 2022 survey by software provider Flexera, companies waste almost one-third—29 percent—of their software spend.

To prevent that waste, the first step is to install, integrate, and customize the technology within your existing infrastructure. None of these technologies work straight out of the box. They have several features, and many of them can be adapted to serve your specific needs. Once the program is set up, you need to actually know how to use the program.

A breakdown in the human system is the most common driver of wasted Martech spending. You can have all the greatest tools, but one simple breakdown can make it all worthless. Take CRM, one of the simpler, more ubiquitous technologies listed here. CRM monitors a prospect's interactions with your company, and almost every other piece of Martech interacts with CRM. For instance, automation software uses CRM data to trigger actions, and ad buy software uses CRM data to target prospects with specific ads. The CRM tool only works if the salesperson properly logs all the data. If they skip steps or use inconsistent coding or forget to input any data at all, the data is ruined and stops the rest of the Martech (and the team) from working.

Software companies realize that their survival relies on customers knowing how to use their products. As such, they provide extensive training and certification programs. Use them. I've seen too many companies convince themselves that they can figure it out on their own. They think a quick one-hour orientation will do the trick, or they dump the user manual on the youngest employee and expect them to figure it out. Neither strategy works and will result in nobody using the technology properly. They don't realize that software requires regular, ongoing investment to maintain, master, and optimize. It's a process, and the sooner companies embrace it, the faster they get the results they want.

PART II

Implement High-Velocity Digital Marketing

CHAPTER 6

Create a High-Velocity Funnel

A sales and marketing funnel models the process of how a company finds prospects and converts them to customers. When implemented effectively, sales and marketing funnels strengthen alignment between sales and marketing teams while making it possible to pinpoint opportunities that improve returns on investments. The funnel is one of the most important parts of marketing. For that reason, whenever I joined a new company as CMO, one of the first things I did was audit its funnel in intimate detail. I almost always needed to revise it. Usually that meant implementing various processes to get everyone on the same page and speaking the same language. Most companies have a funnel in place that is too vague or too complicated to describe.

This complexity is thanks, in part, to SiriusDecisions, now part of Forrester. If you talk about your business's prospects using an ever-growing list of similar-sounding acronyms such as MQLs, SQCs, AQLs, SQOs, and SQAs, or if you dream at night about the mythical quest to measure the demand unit, then you have SiriusDecisions to thank.

Teasing aside, SiriusDecisions was instrumental in the evolution of B2B marketing and sales. In 2002, it became the first to define and articulate the sales and marketing funnel. Marketing leaders, myself included, first operated with an intuitive sense of a funnel (a lot of leads always came in, and far fewer customers came out), SiriusDecisions provided a well-defined template, complete with best practices, for coordinating action and making sense of the chaos of B2B sales and marketing. This played a huge role in my development as a CMO, and you can find SiriusDecisions's fingerprints on almost every B2B organization, whether it knows it or not.

Since 2002, SiriusDecisions has updated and expanded the funnel. Each update adds new details that can be valuable but always introduces more complexity. For all the good it has done, its recommendations have become almost too complicated to implement. Its funnel represents smart thinking by talented analysts. Yet I've personally tried to implement its highly detailed and complicated funnels and have seen many of my peers do the same. None of us had the talent, time, resources, and systems to track and, more importantly, correctly act on everything that a complex funnel models. In fact, most of us found that using more detailed and complicated funnels reduced sales velocity and overall revenue. This occured because extra complexity gives rise to two substantial inefficiencies: acronym soup and too many trees, not enough forest.

1. **Acronym soup:** Every organization creates acronyms to describe its sales and marketing processes, but I rarely see total alignment with what the acronyms mean. More acronyms create more opportunities for miscommunication. Ask ten people on your team to define a qualified sales opportunity (SQO). I bet you'll get many different answers. The best funnels establish a clear, shared language that everyone easily understands and can use. A model with too many

acronyms hinders collaboration as it becomes impossible for people to grasp and use.

2. **Too many trees, not enough forest:** Too many funnels add details that obscure what actually matters. For example, most funnels draw a distinction between a marketing-qualified lead (a lead that marketing has determined is worth selling to) and a sales-qualified lead (a lead that sales has determined is worth selling to). It, of course, matters how many leads pass qualification. At the end of the day, each lead either entered into the pipeline and converted into revenue or it didn't. We only had time to focus on the biggest priorities, and lead conversion into pipeline and revenue mattered far more than how many leads marketing qualified. That's why I recommend simplicity. I'd rather be world-class on the few big things that drive most of my results.

The HVDM Funnel

Over the years, I have developed an HVDM funnel (figure 1) that focuses on the most important processes. It strikes the perfect balance between simple and comprehensive, which makes it much easier to explain to nonmarketers such as CEOs. It shows exactly what to do at each stage of the buyer's journey to move them quickly through the funnel. It builds alignment between marketing and sales by showing exactly where the lead handoff occurs, and it outlines the responsibilities of each group at each stage. Put simply, it links strategy with execution.

Several companies I know have excellent funnels and models but fail to translate those into the real-world results. This funnel shows everyone what to do, when to do it, and how their jobs fit into the whole process. All of this boosts velocity. Because everyone knows what to do, and which of

BUYER'S JOURNEY	SALES & MARKETING PROCESS	STAGE	KEY MEASUREMENTS	HIGH-VELOCITY CONTENT
Discover Has a problem, unaware of solution	• *Owner: Marketing* • Introduce, experience, position, and establish trust	• Inquiry: Ungated Content	• Click-through rates • Website traffic • Bounce rate and duration	• Educational collateral • Educational blogs and videos • Industry benchmarks
Consider Aware of solutions	• *Owner: Marketing until sales accepts lead* • Explain problem—the why • Answer questions on the problem and describe point of view	• Lead: Scored low-high	• Website visitor-to-lead percentage • Total leads • Number and percentage: Low vs. high score	• Free tools • Peer comparison benchmarks
Consideration of specific solutions	• Explain the solution—the how • Answer questions on solution • Establish capabilities	• Sales Accepts Lead: Sales confirms readiness	• Lead-to-sales accepted lead percentage and number • Lead-to-opportunity percentage and number • Number of opportunities	• Free tools • Evaluation criteria reports
Evaluate Decide on best solution	• *Owner: Sales* • Qualification • Differentiation • Present, overcome objections, and propose	• Opportunity: Passes BANT qualification	• Pipeline coverage vs. revenue goal • Lead-to-opportunity velocity	• Product trial • Analyst reports • Success videos
Purchase Solution purchase	• *Owner: Sales* • Close deal	• Close: Win	• Revenue vs. goal • Average deal size • Opportunity-to-deal CVR percentage • New customers added • Lead-to-close CVR percentage and velocity • Customer acquisition cost	• Educational usage videos • Add-on and cross-sell campaigns

$ Revenue

Figure 1

their colleagues rely on them to do their jobs, leads don't languish in limbo. Inquiries get processed, leads get scored faster, and sales only receives sales-ready leads. That means that sales reps get to focus on closing deals with high-quality leads as quickly as possible.

Finally, the funnel is a key component of a complete sales and marketing measurement system. It defines many of the KPIs I use to measure marketing success through the buyer's journey.

I divide the HVDM funnel according to the four stages of the buyer's journey: discover, consider, evaluate, and purchase.

At each stage of the HVDM funnel, I will describe the content that is needed to be developed to build velocity, the key sales and marketing processes, how to code the prospect within the CRM software, and the key measurements at each stage.

Discover

This part of the funnel is primarily marketing's domain. Here, marketing must identify and connect with prospects. This early in the journey, buyers haven't named their problem—they just know the symptoms. They need trusted sources of information to help them verbalize their problem. This means that marketing must create and deploy educational resources and tools that help buyers learn more. At this stage, a prospect merely interacts with ungated content on your website, which makes them an inquiry.

Use Content to Develop Velocity

This early in the buyer's journey, you have a tremendous opportunity. By educating buyers about the problem and why they have the problem, you get to shape the playing field on which all competitors operate. For example, if you know for a fact that you have the easier-to-use product, then in your early funnel educational pieces, you can plant the idea that the best way to solve the problem is with the easiest-to-use solution. That's what we did at Thycotic. Because we had decided to go all in on simplicity, we made sure that our early funnel expert webinars, articles, and blog posts focused on why simplicity mattered. Of course, we did so in a way that provided value. We made sure to define PAM and why it mattered.

But because PAM relies on humans to properly ensure cybersecurity, we dropped in little nuggets that explained why easy-to-use PAM solutions improved cybersecurity. We also knew that one of our primary buyer's titles was system administrator. People in that role manage a huge number of tasks, with security making up a small portion of their job. As a result, they didn't want tools that slowed them down or required lots of training to use. They viewed complexity as evil, and our simplicity-oriented approach resonated with them.

So we deployed a two-pronged messaging approach: simplicity makes systems safer and it requires less work. As an example, in an educational overview of PAM, we mentioned that a staggering number of data breaches because employees don't understand PAM security policies. Then we linked that statement to our PAM Security Policy template, which provides security policy best practices and maps them to key industry regulations. That way buyers could immediately check their policies' quality with a new appreciation of why the policies mattered and how they could be immediately improved.

None of this content was sales-y. But if a customer clicked on our content, they left thinking they wanted something that's intuitive and that their whole company would be able to implement easily and successfully. Then later in the funnel, we showed them our solution's simplicity. It was exactly what they thought they needed because we told them they needed it and the value they'd receive. We created the playing field and earned the right to set ourselves within inches of the goal.

Few things make a prospect understand their problem like a credible industry benchmark. For example, at Thycotic, we created *The State of Password Management*, which showed people how poorly most companies managed their passwords. We didn't just offer high-level information about the differences between strong and weak passwords. Instead, we went into detail, exploring many of the ways companies unintentionally open themselves to attack, such as employees reusing passwords. When our prospects read this, they immediately recognized themselves, saying things like, "Oh, damn. That's us!" Before, they might have suspected they had a problem, but now they could name it, and they knew how much of a risk it represented. Naturally, we showed them how to reach out to us for more information. Try to do the same with your content in this phase and create content that makes people instantly recognize how badly they need your solution.

Essential Marketing and Sales Processes

Most of the work in the marketing stage involves creating sound educational content, making sure that the company is easy to find on Google, and making sure that the content gets to the target audience. In other words, marketing's main responsibility is to design and execute demand generation campaigns, which we cover in great depth in the next chapter.

Marketing can also work on another essential process with sales: outbound prospecting. While it will be the sales reps (or the sales development team) that prospects, the marketing team must assist them. Marketing should always understand the market (including competitors) and the customer—how the customer perceives their challenges and priorities, what keeps them up at night, and what functions they care about the most. This knowledge arms marketing with the information to build a sales-training cadence, providing insight on how to maximize results when prospecting.

Key Measurements

We have already covered a number of these key measurements, namely, organic traffic rates, total website traffic, and web CVR, in chapters three and four (the Google and website chapters). In addition to those measurements, I've used three other metrics to determine success in the discover phase:

1. **Number of net new inquiries by source:** Success in this metric varies depending on business size, but almost always, the more, the better. I always broke them down by source (for example, email campaign, PPC ad, or organic traffic). This gave me a better sense of which marketing techniques performed best, so I would know where to invest more in future quarters.

2. **Inquiry-to-lead CVR:** This tracks the percentage of inquiries that become leads. A low inquiry-to-lead CVR means poor discover content, low-quality inquiries, or both. Low-quality inquiries indicate that marketing's messages are not reaching or resonating with the right people. Success in this metric varies from industry to industry, but few companies see more than 5 percent of their total inquiries convert.

3. **Digital ad click-through rates:** Digital ad click-through rates show the number of clicks an ad receives divided by the number of times the ad runs. It is used to measure how well your keywords and ads are performing. I used this to show which ads and keywords produced the most inquiries so I could increase my investment in them and phase out the low-performing ad buys.

Consider

Marketing owns this part of the funnel. In this stage, prospects already understand what's bothering them in great detail and begin to think about solutions. At this point, prospects do not necessarily evaluate solution providers. Instead, they look for types of options available to them. For example, someone with an old couch at this phase is trying to decide whether they should get it reupholstered or buy a new couch altogether. During this stage in marketing, a prospect usually fills out a form in exchange for content they consider valuable, which makes them a lead.

Use Content to Develop Velocity

Focus on building content that shows why your solution is best. Free tools with limited capability often demonstrate this perfectly. What I call live-for collaterals also work well. These are sample reports or sample outputs from your product that shows a prospect what they would get if they bought from you. For example, if a company sells accounting software, they could create a paper called *The Top Ten Compliance Reports CFOs Live For*. They would populate the document with samples of the reports that their software produces. In my live-fors, I showcased the full range of my product's best capabilities. I chose examples that illustrated how customers could customize the software to fit the needs of their business, how they could easily access the critical information they needed, and, of course, how they could quickly generate a report to submit to a government body or a CFO.

I've found that peer comparison benchmarks tend to perform well. Keep in mind that you're not just competing against other companies, you're also competing against the status quo. These benchmarks show how a prospect's current practices or results compare to others in their peer group.

For example, we created a free tool at Thycotic called the Privileged Password Vulnerability Benchmark, which companies used to understand how their password management practices stacked up. Often, they would see that they lagged behind. It made them realize that their status quo wasn't sustainable, and if they didn't want their competitors to have an advantage, they should consider our solution. Prospects loved these type of tools, and lead volume went off the charts.

Lead-Scoring Processes

After marketing brings in the leads, they must evaluate them. They do this through a process called lead scoring. The goal of lead scoring is to assess where a lead is in the buying cycle and if they are likely to buy or not. Each lead receives a score based on various criteria such as their job title or recent online behavior. The hottest leads get the highest scores and get sent straight to the sales team. The colder leads receive lower scores and stay with marketing. Marketing follows up with a combination of emails and targeted ads until the lead receives a high enough score to go to the sales team or becomes dormant or disqualified.

In a business of any sort of scale, it is impossible to lead score without automation. We discussed many tools that help with lead scoring in chapter five (Martech). That being said, you still need to know how to use the tool. There are two key steps for setting up a successful automated lead-scoring model: select and weight lead-score criteria and determine target scores.

Select and Weight Lead-Score Criteria

First you need to understand what criteria you will use to evaluate prospects. There are two basic types of criteria: explicit and implicit.

Explicit criteria are information that the prospect intentionally provides such as the information on a filled out registration form on your website. This is raw data before it's been analyzed or interpreted. Here are some examples of explicit criteria:

- Company name
- Location

- Business type or industry
- Revenue
- Number of employees
- Lead source
- Title or job role
- Past purchases

Implicit criteria, on the other hand, isn't provided. Instead, it comes from the analysis of either the explicit data or the prospect's online behavior. The implicit data reveals much more about whether a prospect is ready to buy, and if they are, it reveals what stage of the buying process they are in. It also helps the salespeople know exactly what content each lead engaged with, allowing them to tailor their follow-up based on the information in that content. Here are some examples of implicit criteria:

- **Visits to your website:** Number of pages visited, frequency and length of visits
- **Phone calls:** Both inbound and outbound
- **Content interactions:** Downloads of white papers, videos, podcasts, and infographics
- **Subscriptions:** Requests for newsletters and RSS feeds
- **Webinar attendance:** Number of webinars registered for and attended, and webinar topics
- **Website form completions:** For demos, contact, surveys, questionnaires
- **Off-line events:** Trade shows and seminars

I used three guiding lights to select and weight criteria: the ideal buyer persona, input from the sales team, and empirical data. The closer that a lead is to your ideal buyer persona, the more likely they are to buy, so put a lot of weight on any characteristic that matches that persona. Since the sales team has the best sense of what a high-quality lead looks like and ultimately closes the deals, I gave extra weight to any characteristics they highlighted.

Finally, I weighted implicit data and behavior based on past CVRs for similar activities. For example, if I knew that a high percentage of the people who downloaded a specific free tool eventually converted to revenue, I would design my model so that almost anybody who downloaded the tool went straight to sales. Or if somebody attended an early stage webinar, I would design the model so that activity alone would not send them to sales. But if they downloaded a white paper, visited our website several times, searched for best PAM solutions for aviation companies, and several people from the same company IP address started to visit the website, indicating that they desperately want to buy, I would weight my lead-scoring criteria so that prospect would go to sales even though they never downloaded or interacted with late-stage content.

Conversely, I knew that most of our trade show leads never converted. A lot of people at trade shows drop their email for a nice tchotchke, not because they want to buy.

Let's look at an example. I usually use a scale of -3 to 10 points, with the most desirable characteristics and behaviors getting a 10, and the least getting either a 0 or a negative score. The matrix in figure 2 shows how I would weight characteristics from prospects in four criteria: job position, department, company size, and type of company. To keep my lead-scoring example simple, I used only four categories:

- Best: 10 points
- Second Best: 6 points
- Third Best: 3 points
- Worst: 0 points

DEMOGRAPHIC	LEAD INPUT	SCORE
Job Level/Seniority	VP	+ Most points (10)
	Director	+ 2nd most points (6)
	Manager	+ Few points (3)
Most Important Factor for Fictional Company	HR	+ Most points (10)
	Finance	+ 2nd most points (6)
	Legal	+ Few points (3)
Employee Size	500–999	+ Most points (10)
	999–5,000	+ 2nd most points (6)
	250–499	+ Few points (3)
Company Type	B2B	+ Most points (10)
	B2C	+ 2nd most points (6)
	Nonprofit	- Negative points (-3)

Figure 2: Sample lead-scoring matrix for B2B businesses

Determine the Target Score

Leads accrue points over time, and as soon as they reach a certain threshold of points, they go to the sales team. You need to carefully set the points threshold to send leads to sales. This is a massively important part of the process. If you set the threshold too high, plenty of hot leads languish in the system and buy from someone else. If you set the threshold too low, a wave of cold or unqualified leads will inundate the sales team.

There is no perfect lead-score threshold. Almost any number will inevitably exclude some qualified leads, let some poor leads through, and often will even do both. For that reason, experiment with the thresholds. Pay attention to the metrics to see if different factors deserve different priority in the model. Listen to what sales says. If they gripe about too many crummy leads, raise the threshold. If they close almost everything they get and gripe about not getting enough leads, lower the threshold. This skill only comes from practice and careful observation.

If you're just getting started, however, there is a simple methodology that will point you in the right direction. First, add up the highest score a prospect can get. Then choose a few of the most important or desirable traits that a prospect might have that would indicate they are a high-quality lead. For example, it might be their role, the size of their company, the industry they work in, or the amount of content they've interacted with. If they score a 10 for each of those traits, then their score would come out to 40. The table below shows a scenario like that.

SAMPLE LEAD-SCORE DESCRIPTIONS		
Lead Score	**Lead Type**	**Description**
0–29	Lead (Low score)	Prospect is in the exploration phase. They might have downloaded content for educational purposes or might have lost points for inactivity.
30–59	Lead (Medium score)	Prospect has executed some combination of favorable activities and shared valuable demographic information but has not passed full qualification yet.
60+	Lead (High score)	Prospect is ready for the sales team! They likely show a mix of the right persona-based factors paired with plenty of behavior that shows intent to buy.

In this example, even with a perfect 10 across several categories, the lead still isn't ready for sales. But if they revisit the website, download a white paper, or respond to an email or a PPC ad, then that might be enough to push them over 60 points and to the sales team.

Key Measurements

Key metrics to track include:

Number of net new leads: Success depends on several factors, including the strength of content, SEO work, and ad campaigns. In many ways, the number of new leads indicates whether the top half of your funnel is performing as well as it should. The more new leads gained per quarter, the better for business as long as you have a lead-scoring model in place.

Total leads by source: Tracking this metric will prove invaluable. It will show exactly which activities in marketing produce the most leads and revenue. This gets tricky, too, as most leads encounter several touchpoints. For example, somebody might find the website via an organic search, then come back after clicking a YouTube ad. Whenever possible, source the lead by the first touchpoint. That will give a far more accurate picture of how each strategy performs. The following are examples of how to classify lead sources:

- Search
  — Organic
  — AdWords
- Referral
  — Customer
  — Partner
  — Employee
- Web referral (traffic sent from another website)
  — Referring website
- Social
  — Twitter
  — LinkedIn
  — Facebook

- Advertising (paid media)
  — Specific display ad campaigns
- Sponsored content (paid media)
  — Specific content download
  — Specific sponsored webinar
- Events
  — Specific event
- Business development
  — Tele-prospecting

Percentage of leads by lead score: This metric reveals the quality of leads that you generate. You want as many leads as possible to come in with a high lead score right off the bat. Hotter leads convert to revenue more quickly. Too many leads with low scores indicate a problem with marketing strategy. You typically either need to change the messaging, where you place the ads, or the offer. Also pay attention to trends in lead scores by source, as that information will tell you where the best leads come from and allow you to improve your overall ROI.

Total and percentage of leads that sales accepts: If sales thinks that a lead has a strong chance to convert, they accept the lead. At this point, ownership of the lead transfers from marketing to sales. A high percentage of sales-accepted leads indicates that the lead-scoring threshold is in the right place. In addition to tracking the CVR, you should also track the total numbers of leads and sales-accepted leads to see if they are growing.

Evaluate

The sales team owns most of the responsibility for this part of the funnel, though marketing plays an important role. By now, the prospect knows most everything about their problem and the best type of solution for them. At this point, they evaluate different providers and decided who to buy from. Therefore, their questions during this stage will focus on your product and company. Here are some questions they may ask:

- Why are you better than a competitor?
- What type of warranty do you offer?
- What are the contract terms?
- What are the pricing options?
- How does your product handle my specific case?

They will ask most of these questions during conversations with sales reps. If those conversations go well and the lead seems particularly hot, then it is during this phase that they will become an opportunity.

Use Content to Develop Velocity

The best content at this stage helps to close the deal. Most B2B buys represent a significant investment. Because people typically spend on must-have solutions, they usually feel like their choice needs to be 100 percent right. Because of that, they will be careful and deliberate. Any content that builds confidence will help.

In my experience, the most important sort of content for this stage are free trials paired with video guides for the trials. I also recommend delivering third-party analyst reports that cover the differences between you and your competitors and align with your messaging. Prospects often trust analysts more than marketers and salespeople, and leading your prospects to analyst-written reports will go a long way toward establishing trust and credibility. I always like to have reports from three different types of analysts: the major firms, independent analysts, and peer insight groups.

The major firms such as Gartner and Forrester regularly research almost every industry and interview customers about their experience and companies about their products. They compile the data and interviews and give recommendations based on their research. Prospects consider these reports the gold standard. However, even within these large firms, some analysts have better reputations than others. Work to get favorable coverage from the most trusted analysts.

To get featured in the reports requires a significant investment of time and energy. You need to know which analysts are working on what reports and when. At Thycotic, I called analysts and asked them when their reports were due and added each deadline to a calendar. Then I created an engagement strategy that would make sure we got covered in the reports. That strategy usually included reaching out regularly to establish a rapport with the analysts. They don't mind these sorts of conversations—in fact, they rely on them to do their jobs. They need to see internal documents and materials from each major player in an industry. To do that, they need access.

A close relationship with analysts has several other benefits. Analysts talk to customers as much as, if not more than, they talk to sellers. If you have a strong relationship with an analyst, then they're more likely to mention you to customers. Most firms require analysts to track how often they mention each vendor. I would receive reports about how often they brought us up, and if our mentions dropped, then we would reestablish contact.

We also learned a lot from our conversations with analysts. Sometimes they would let slip a bit of valuable information about one of our competitors that we could capitalize on. They're not supposed to do that, but it happens. We are all human. We could also ask the analysts for their honest thoughts on aspects of our business. We sometimes got amazing ideas from them, such as for content, new products, or new features. Whenever we did, we gave them full credit. It's a relationship. We wanted to do whatever we could to maintain it.

You can also commission a report from analysts, though they tend to be pricey. A benefit, however, is that you can often use these reports in a lead generation campaign. Prospects want access to these reports because they provide important industry-wide insights for buyers and come from a credible source. They will often give their personal information to get them.

Finally, some analysts offer to compile peer insights and user reviews into single reports that can be purchased. Think Amazon reviews but aggregated and analyzed. Sometimes these can prove more useful than other types of reports. They cut straight to the issues that matter the most to any potential buyer: whether the product will work for them and the unique needs of their organization, make their life easier, and whether their peers get the kind of results the potential buyer wants to achieve.

Along the same vein, at every company I've worked for, we recruited current customers to help us close deals either by appearing in customer success videos or by serving as references. Because customer intimacy was a core part of our culture, we never ran out of eager volunteers.

At Thycotic, we strove to have a customer champion to represent each type of customer we served, so that we always had somebody who could speak to the unique challenges of a prospect. We recruited customers from small, medium, and large businesses and from each of the main industries who used each product and used them for different reasons. This can take a lot of time, depending on the size of the company. Managing these testimonials and references alone can be a full-time job. But it builds velocity, and if you do it well, you'll be ready with a reference whenever a prospect needs one.

Granted, this is a lot of content. The goal is to create an overwhelming wall of validation, anything to make a customer feel confident investing in your company. Don't worry if you don't have all of this right away. Just make a commitment to get started, knowing that a lot of the content you create around customer satisfaction will have a long shelf life. Focus on building as many of these reports as possible. A gap in this part of the funnel is particularly painful. You've already gotten your lead all the way to the altar; you don't want them to flee the chapel right before they say I do.

Essential Sales and Marketing Processes

In this phase, the marketing team provides content that showcases the unique benefits of your product or solution, such as product trials, frequently asked questions pages, live demos, side-to-side competitive feature analysis, and customer success videos.

At the same time, the sales team steps in and performs their magic. First, they need to qualify the lead further. The best way to do this is with a discovery phone call. Don't think of this as a sales call but instead as a casual business conversation that will help both parties decide if they should move forward. For this call, I recommend IBM's BANT qualification, which holds that a sales-qualified lead meets three of these four BANT criteria:

1. **Budget:** Does the prospect have the budget to buy the product?
2. **Authority:** Does the prospect have the decision-making authority or are they an influencer?
3. **Need:** Does the prospect have a business need for the product?
4. **Time frame:** Will the prospect be implementing a solution in a suitable time frame?

After a prospect becomes an opportunity, sales adds them to the pipeline. A pipeline is generally expressed in terms of dollar value or by how much revenue each opportunity is expected to generate. But not every opportunity is equal. Some are much closer to closing than others.

To create an accurate forecast of how much revenue you will produce in a given quarter, you need to assign different values to different opportunities, depending on how far along they are in the process. For example, at Thycotic, we weighted opportunities in five stages: open opportunity, active project, shortlist, forecast, and close win.

Stage 1: Open Opportunity

At this stage, we enter 10 percent of the total projected contract into the pipeline. To do that, the following must be true:

- We have established two-way contact with the prospect.
- We understand the prospect's pain point and have a solution to address it.
- The prospect is interested in a solution to solve their pain.
- We and the prospect have agreed on a next step.
- We have the basic contact information and understand the relationship dynamics with the buyer, decision maker, and decision influencers.

Stage 2: Active Project

At this stage, we enter 30 percent of the total projected revenue of the contract into the pipeline, and the following must be true:

- The buying process is ongoing or will start in ninety days.
- We know the specific pain of the decision maker (not just the company) and what they stand to gain from our product.
- We understand the buying time frame and have found a way to create urgency with the prospect.
- We know the prospect has the budget to purchase our product.
- We understand what the prospect requires.
- We know who our competitors are for this client.
- We have provided an initial price quote.
- We have delivered a live demo.
- A free trial has been initiated or scheduled.

Stage 3: Shortlist

At this stage, we enter 60 percent of the total projected contract into the pipeline, and the following must be true:

- We are a finalist for the contract, or some competitors have been eliminated.
- The prospect acknowledges that our solution meets their needs.
- We have presented a quote to the person who will sign the contract.
- We are actively negotiating pricing.

Stage 4: Forecast

At this stage, we enter 85 percent of the total projected contract into the pipeline, and the following must be true:

- The prospect provides verbal commitment that we are the chosen solution.
- We have established a mutually defined and agreed upon closing plan and date.
- Pricing and contract negotiations are in the final stages or complete.
- The contract is pending, requiring sign-off by all authorities.
- We are awaiting the order.

Stage 5: Close Win

At this stage, we enter 100 percent of the actual value of the contract as revenue, rather than to the pipeline, and the following must be true:

- We won the business.

/////

While, traditionally, sales teams handle this part of the qualification process, I've found that creating a team completely dedicated to performing this level of qualification can increase velocity. At Thycotic, we called these employees business development representatives (BDRs), but some companies call them sales development representatives. Essentially, we would send the leads who scored the highest during the qualification stage straight to the sales account executives. Those were rock-solid leads, and we wanted to get them to our best salespeople as quickly as possible. The lowest-rated leads stayed with the marketing team for a process known as lead nurturing (more about that in the next chapter). The midlevel leads went to the BDRs to go through the BANT qualification. The BDRs would then pass the best leads along to the sales account executives and knock the lower-rated leads back down to marketing. In this distribution of labor, marketing markets, sales sells, and the junior BDRs develop more qualified leads.

This was the most efficient system I've worked with. In many organizations, salespeople waste tons of time qualifying poor leads. The BDRs freed up our top sales reps to close more high-value deals. Plus, the BDRs created a great farm system for new sales talent. At Thycotic, we hired young people for the BDR team who were eager to break into sales. Then we would track their performance. We promoted the highest-performing ones to full sales reps. It's better to promote from within for these sorts of roles because established employees already understand the products, our company, our ideal client, and don't require a lot of additional training to sell effectively. In periods of rapid growth, when we would suddenly need a whole host of new sales personnel, we pulled first from the BDR team before scrambling to hire outside talent.

After the lead has been qualified, it becomes an opportunity. Opportunities enter into the sales pipeline and typically become part of the company's sales forecast. From then on, sales focuses on overcoming objections and ensuring that the salespeople have a unique selling proposition that sets the company and its products above the competitive alternatives. Finally, proposals are presented, negotiation occurs, and ideally the salespeople win the business. It's important to note that rarely do these processes happen in a nice, neat sequential order. Nevertheless, a deep understanding of the process helps salespeople handle situations when they become chaotic in the real world.

Key Measurements

The top metrics to track include:

The percentage and total number of leads that convert into opportunities: The percentage of leads that convert to opportunities reflects the quality of leads that marketing generates. In addition to tracking the CVR, you should also track the total number of leads and opportunities to see if they grow.

The total number and value of opportunities created in each period: This metric focuses on the number and dollar value of opportunities reflected in your sales pipeline.

The dollar value of the pipeline vs. the revenue goal: Sales pipeline coverage measures the ratio between the dollar value of your pipeline and upcoming revenue targets. This is calculated by dividing your pipeline by how much quota you need to close. The rule of thumb is to have three to four times more pipeline than quota.

Lead-to-opportunity velocity: This metric measures the time (expressed in days) it takes a lead to convert to an opportunity.

Sold

You won the business, wahoo! However, your work is by no means done. More processes must take place.

Processes

The marketing or customer success teams need to continue to produce and deliver content to make sure the customer gets the value they paid for, renews, and, ideally, buys more.

Use Content to Develop Velocity

Content in this stage usually takes two forms: First, a welcome package to thank the customer and offer resources to improve their onboarding and initial experience. Second, videos or an easy-to-follow manual that shows customers how to use what they bought. Eventually, you can remarket content that showcases related products to these customers. Unless you want to annoy your newly acquired customer, don't send any new offers until they've received real value from their original purchase.

Key Measurements

Key metrics to track include:

Revenue vs. revenue goal: This measures the actual revenue delivered against the company's revenue target for a given time. Most companies also measure the actual revenue against the total assigned quota as well as the historical performance for both.

New customers added: Total new customers in each period as well as historical performance.

Average Sales Price (ASP): If you sell thousands of software licenses at different prices, you calculate the ASP by dividing the total revenue earned from licensed sales by the number of licenses sold.

Opportunity-to-deal CVR: Opportunity CVR is the ratio of sales closed within a given time versus the open pipeline at the start of the period.

Opportunity-to-deal velocity: The number of days it takes for an opportunity to convert into a deal.

End-to-end conversion rate, or win rate: The percent of leads that convert into customers.

End-to-end deal velocity: The number of days it takes for a lead to convert into a deal.

Customer acquisition cost (CAC): CAC is calculated by dividing all the costs of acquiring customers (marketing and sales expenses) by the number of customers acquired in the period the money was spent. CAC helps determine a company's profitability: the lower the acquisition cost, the more profit the company gets from each customer.

CHAPTER 7

Set Revenue Goals

Does this sound familiar? An executive sets a revenue target, then everyone guesses how many leads and opportunities they need to generate to hit that number. Marketing puts together an equation that goes something like the number of leads needed multiplied by the estimated cost per lead. This spits out a massive budget that the CEO would never go for. So marketing takes the budget they're given and tells everybody to buckle down or do more with less. Then they run their campaigns and hope for the best. Sometimes this black magic works. More often than not, it fails spectacularly.

This goal-setting method fails because it lacks the empirical data needed to consistently make accurate estimates, and it only measures performance at one part of the funnel—the top. With this limited approach, a company might generate the right number of leads but still fall short on revenue. That failure comes from a lack of understanding of the incremental metrics they need to hit in order to reach the target. For example, do they know their lead-to-opportunity CVR? How does that impact their ability to reach the revenue mark? What does a 10 percent decrease in CVR do to the bottom line? How would they know that the rate dropped, and, more importantly, how would they fix it?

Because most organizations only look at leads and revenue, the leaders pound their desks and demand more leads when a CVR drops. But that often doesn't solve the actual problem—you can get all the leads in the world, but if they don't *convert*, you won't get the revenue. It's an imprecise model, and precision in planning always produces better results.

Model Building for Precision

In my experience, that precision comes from a bottom-up, data-driven revenue sourcing model. This sort of model breaks down revenue goals into individual steps. It shows exactly how many leads and opportunities and how much revenue the sales, marketing, and channel teams need to produce each quarter, and reveals the levers they can pull to reach those marks.

In business, the ability to create an accurate model like this is an outright superpower. It enables you to have productive, intelligent conversations with the CEO and other top brass. For example, let's say the CEO pushes for arbitrary and, according to the empiric data, unreasonable revenue targets. With this model, you can explain why the objectives are too high and then start a conversation that leads to more achievable goals. I'm not suggesting you start an argument with your CEO or use the model as an excuse not to push yourself and perform. The point merely is that if you're like me, you may need a way to create a conversation about what realistic growth looks like and what resources you need to achieve it.

When I had those conversations and then consistently delivered the growth that my model predicted, I earned the trust of the board members I worked for and the senior leaders I worked with. It can be the same for you. At Thycotic, this model ultimately helped us understand exactly what we needed to deliver. The clarity helped us achieve our quarterly revenue targets for nearly six straight years—and we didn't set modest targets by any means. Most years we achieved 35–50 percent year-over-year revenue growth, and occasionally we set the goal even higher and attained it. You can create your own revenue sourcing model in two steps by capturing and categorizing revenue data and by calculating CVRs for each step of the sales cycle.

Step One: Capture and Categorize Revenue Data

When building your revenue sourcing model from scratch, start with the company's historical, quarter-by-quarter performance. Break down the company's revenue into the categories that make the most sense. In the technology world, we classify revenue in three ways: new, upsell or cross-sell, and renewal.

Next, break down the revenue by the functional department (marketing, sales, or channel partner, for example) that sourced each deal. When I say *sourced*, I mean who made the first contact, not the last contact. Some companies I've advised define sourcing based on the last department to touch a prospect. Because sales or channel partners almost always close deals and therefore touch the prospect last, that approach obfuscates marketing's performance. This can get tricky if, say, a prospect responded to a PPC ad years ago, went dormant, and then suddenly reactivated during a prospecting call with a salesperson. In this case, I would say that sales sourced the lead because they had first contact in the relevant time frame.

Then I suggest breaking down the revenue even further into whatever categories make sense for your business. The more granular the categories, the better. For example, if you sell only one product but sell to buyers in several geographies, then break the revenue down by major geographic region. If you sell several products across all geographies, as we did at Thycotic, then break the revenue down by product type within each geographic region.

Most companies should have this data available. However, in extreme cases the data might be hard to get. When that happens, gather senior leaders from the sales, marketing, and channel partners teams and attempt together to reverse engineer the numbers.

Step Two: Calculate the CVRs for Each Step of the Sales Cycle

Once you have categorized your revenue, the second step is to determine the opportunity, lead, and inquiry volume and the CVRs that led to that revenue. This is a bottom-up model so we start at the end of the journey with revenue and deals needed and work backward from there. Let's examine a super simplified model so you can see how the planning works.

Determine the Opportunities Needed to Reach Revenue Targets

For each category outlined in step one, calculate the average size of each deal. This will tell you how many deals you need to reach your revenue goals. For example, if your goal for new business is $1,000, and each deal is worth $100 dollars, you need ten new deals. In this example, we aren't dealing with upsells and renewals, so you will need to go through a similar process for upsells and renewals if its applicable to your business.

Then, to figure out how many opportunities you need to create, calculate the opportunity-to-deal CVR using your latest CVR. For example:

- Opportunity-to-deal CVR: 40 percent
- Opportunities needed: 25

Now you know how many deals and opportunities you need to hit your new business revenue target of $1,000. Next, you need to assign a target number of deals and opportunities to each functional department so they know what they are on the hook for. For simplicity, let's assume that this company doesn't have channel partners, and they expect sales and marketing each to source the same number of deals. In reality, you probably won't expect sales and marketing to come up with the same number of deals. Marketing usually is responsible for sourcing most deals, and you want to assign these targets based on recent performance.

- Deals sourced by:
  — Sales: 5
  — Marketing: 5
- Opportunities required by functional department:
  — Sales: 12
  — Marketing: 13

Determine the Leads Needed to Source Opportunities

Next, figure out how many leads you need each functional department to create. To do this, first calculate the lead-to-opportunity CVR from the previous year's numbers.

- Opportunities needed: 25
- Lead-to-opportunity CVR: 25 percent
- Total leads needed: 100
- Leads required from each functional department:
  — Sales: 50
  — Marketing: 50

Determine the Inquiries Required to Source Leads

Next, use the most recent inquiry-to-lead conversion rate to calculate the number of inquiries you need to create the leads required. Keep in mind that the conversion rates typically vary from tactic to tactic. For example, organic traffic usually converts at a much higher rate than PPC ads, and both of those tactics perform better than display ads. Again, the more granular, the better, so for best results calculate the inquiry-to-lead conversion rate for each source:

- Leads needed: 100
- Overall inquiry-to-lead conversion rate: 3 percent
- Total inquiries needed: 3,333
- Inquiries sourced from: (I've done this arbitrarily. In reality, you should use the empiric data and work with the marketing team to decide how each tactic will contribute to the 3,333 required inquiries.)
  — Search: 1,500
    - Organic: 1,000
    - AdWords: 500
  — Social: 500
    - Twitter: 200
    - LinkedIn: 275
    - Facebook: 25
  — Advertising (paid media): 1,000
    - Campaign A: 500
    - Campaign B: 500
  — Sponsored Content: 333
    - Specific sponsored webinars: 333

Work the Model and Make the Model Work

Once you have the model set up, you have to actually use it and let it guide your processes and decisions. There are two primary ways that I use the model to ensure the marketing plan contributes to the attainment of revenue objectives: first, measure marketing performance and optimize strategy and tactics and second, manage and motivate my team.

Optimize Marketing Strategy

Once you've implemented a marketing strategy, the model will help you measure performance and optimize each piece of your operation. Ideally, you create a dashboard that shows how company performance compares to goals in real time. Then you can check the assumptions that you made in the planning process against what is actually happening. Maybe PPC ads convert at a higher rate than expected, so you decide to invest more in them. Or PPC might underperform. You will be able to see any inefficiencies instantly.

Then troubleshoot and correct the problem, or find opportunities to make up for the underperformance elsewhere. For example, if I notice that our PPC underperformed, I might look at our landing pages to see if we could improve them. Or I would look deeper to see which keywords that we placed ads on performed better than others. If I didn't see a way to boost our numbers, I would shift the budget to a tactic that was doing better and capitalize on that momentum.

Optimizing investments also helps keep CAC down. A company's target CAC depends on several factors. Start-ups need to invest a substantial amount of money to establish themselves in the market, and they tend to spend more money to acquire each customer than larger companies. Therefore, many people don't pay too much attention to CAC early in a company's development. Instead, they obsess over capturing market share, thinking that they will eventually bring in enough volume to overcome high customer acquisition costs.

But the spend-bunches-to-build-market-share approach never made sense to me or Jim Legg, the CEO of Thycotic. We believed, as Jim put it, that we should run a business like a business—in other words, in a capital-efficient manner. While we allowed for a higher CAC early on, we made sure it didn't get astronomical. We knew that the obsession with market share, CAC and monetization strategy be damned, contributed (in part) to the dot-com crash. The obsession created a host of companies that were burning through cash without a path to profitability. This was not sustainable.

Watching so many companies flame out so quickly served as a powerful warning. For that reason, I like to cap CAC at about 25 percent of the average lifetime value of each customer. This is especially important if you hope to go public, sell to a private equity firm, or get acquired by a larger competitor. Almost any investor or buyer will closely examine CAC before they make an offer. The shift from a growth focus to a profitability focus will always pose challenges, but it's easier if CAC never gets out of hand in the first place.

Manage and Motivate Your Team

Before joining Thycotic, Jim Legg and I had worked together for many years at two different start-ups. In that time, we hit our revenue goals for more than sixty quarters in a row. Most people are amazed when they hear this. They assume that somewhere along the line, something outside of our control must have happened that prevented us from surpassing our goals. But it never happened.

We weren't always just strolling down a nice meadow path, though. A couple of times, something did threaten our ability to make our quarterly numbers. But each time we managed to overcome the challenges and hit or exceed our targets. Part of this success came from implementing the processes and methods described in this book. We would also carefully research each company before we agreed to work there. We wanted to make sure that the company was well positioned in a growing market and that it had a product we believed in.

That being said, a large part of our success came from the accountability that our revenue model drove and demanded. First of all, the senior leaders all signed off on the goals at the start of the quarter. This meant that we agreed among ourselves to be fully accountable for the leads, opportunites, and revenue we needed to reach our goals. The chiefs of each department would report weekly to the CEO on their progress. This kept us aligned at the highest levels. Because the model broke down revenue targets into hyper-specific smaller goals, senior leadership was able to help the staff succeed by ensuring everyone understood the baby steps they needed to take to achieve the goals.

We also encouraged our employees to own their goals and responsibilities in part by pinning quarterly bonuses to hitting the targets. This is where the magic happened. Suddenly, even our social media staff abandoned judging success based on how much engagement each post gets and instead tracked how they contributed to the pipeline and revenue instead. While we never expected the social media staff to produce the same level of revenue as our PPC advertising, we still identified the portion of revenue they were responsible for. Ditto our trade show teams.

Trade shows, while analog, still make up an important part of a HVDM process. They can be a good source of leads, which you can funnel into digital marketing programs and eventually turn into revenue. Yet far too many companies treat trade shows as distinct from their digital marketing and barely view trade shows as an opportunity to grow revenue. When I advise companies and ask about how recent trade shows went, people say things like, "Great! The CEO came, we gave a lot of talks, it was a lot of fun. We made some good new contacts." When I ask them how many leads they produced, how much pipeline and revenue came out of the show, I get astounded looks.

In my career, we had trade shows down to a science. Everyone who participated knew exactly how we defined success and what they needed to do to help us achieve it. They knew they needed to get a specific number of leads each day, give a specific number of product demonstrations, or have a certain number of customer meetings. I tied bonuses to all of these metrics but also made the bonuses dependent on team performance. That way we reaped the benefits of peer pressure. Everyone had to hit their individual goals for everyone else to be rewarded. It helped those involved with each event to hold one another accountable and helped us maximize our return on investment.

This focus on how everyone in marketing contributes to revenue completely changed how our staff approached their jobs. They could refer to the model to coordinate and focus their efforts. If something went wrong, anybody involved in sales or marketing could at any moment recognize and diagnose the problem. Maybe, for some reason, our leads weren't converting to the pipeline at the rate we expected. Or maybe we weren't getting enough inquiries to the website. Sometimes the digital marketing would deliver a huge number of well-qualified leads to the sales team. But since the digital marketing team needed to hit revenue and opportunity-sourcing metrics, and not just lead metrics, they cared about whether or not the sales team closed those leads. So the digital marketing team would track how long it took for sales to follow up. If it took too long, the digital marketing team would be all over them.

All this contributes to a high-achieving culture. Everyone knows what's important. They see how their jobs connect with everyone elses, and they work together to grow revenue. It helps them prioritize work and solve problems proactively with little oversight. I didn't have to be everywhere at once, which gave me the time I needed to focus on our overall stragey, our content, and how we positioned ourselves in the market. This is what every CMO should want. I still monitored the metrics myself and intervened and offered support whenever necessary. We had regular meetings, and I congratulated people on their performance, gave accolades when employees took initiative to make sure we stayed on track, and held people accountable when they didn't reach their goals.

I used to ask people what they thought my favorite color was. They'd guess red, blue, purple, green. I'd tell them, "No. My favorite color is clear." This is because when success measures are clear, and when everyone knows exactly what they need to do to contribute to the overall revenue goals, miraculous things are possible.

CHAPTER 8

Build High-Velocity Demand Generation Campaigns

John Wanamaker, the nineteenth-century founder of the Wanamaker's department store, famously said: "Half the money I spend on advertising is wasted; the trouble is I don't know which half." He was talking about newspaper advertising, but the quote still applies to contemporary companies' experiences with advertising. In fact, a company that takes an old-fashioned approach to its online marketing would be lucky to waste only half of their money.

The internet has totally disrupted advertising. You cannot approach a digital demand generation campaign in the way people used to approach TV, print, and radio advertising. It's not enough to come up with an interesting spot and drop it on the best channels. Success on the internet requires a comprehensive set of highly targeted demand generation campaigns, where you have seconds to capture a buyer's attention. Before designing campaigns, you need to identify clear audience segments and create cohesive content stories.

Identify Clear Audience Segments

Audience segmentation is the process of dividing your target audience into specific subgroups (segments) that you can target with unique campaigns. Old-school marketers almost always segment their audiences based on demographic indicators. For example, if they sell workflow management software, they put all the middle IT managers in one bucket, the IT executives in another, and the IT professionals in a third. Some build campaigns that target each group. Others use the same campaign for all three groups. Both approaches waste money and undermine profitability.

Google's research shows that campaigns based solely on demographic targeting risk missing more than 70 percent of potential mobile shoppers. Why? Because targeting someone based on their job title will get a message to the right person but not always at the right time. A high-velocity approach targets prospects who show clear intent to buy. As Lisa Gevelber, the CMO of the Americas Region at Google, puts it, "Intent beats identity. Immediacy trumps loyalty."

My approach is to divide each buyer persona into groups based on whether they are looking to buy. Then I further divide the in-market prospects based on what part of the sales and marketing funnel they are in. To determine which group a potential buyer falls into, I look at their internet history, including what pieces of my company's content they've engaged with, what they've searched for, and the web pages they've visited. For example, an IT executive watching an introductory webinar on YouTube is likely in the discovery phase because they are trying to learn more about a problem. A business leader signing up to get a thirty-day trial of software is showing stronger intent because they are in the evaluation phase, trying out software, which indicates they are closer to making a purchase decision. And someone who hasn't even sniffed around in my niche probably doesn't want to buy anything at all.

Another way to get this kind of valuable information is to use a third-party vendor to acquire cookie data from people in your target audience. You can use Google Trends to track search trends and queries in your category. To maximize velocity, I recommend keeping your cookie and tracking windows to thirty days or shorter, so your tracking efforts are more likely to target people with a current interest in your company. This will tell you what people are looking for and how much information each prospect has processed. From there, you can categorize them and design hyper-specific campaigns. You can feed an IT executive who searches for *password management software educational* early funnel content and feed late-funnel content to an executive who watches one of your webinars. Done correctly, you know exactly who to target and when, and how to feed them compelling communication—all of which accelerates the sales cycle.

Create Cohesive Content Stories

A successful high-velocity demand generation campaign provides real value to the customer at each stage of the buying process. To provide value effectively, each part of the customer journey requires its own content. More than that, the content must fit together to create a cohesive story. Each piece of content should nudge the prospect down the funnel toward a purchase. I recommend mapping your content for each product and audience segment to the customer journey. Building these diagrams will take time in the beginning but will enable you to see any gaps so you can build content to fill them and improve velocity. Here's a simple example diagram from Thycotic:

Figure 3

Over time, you will create several pieces of content for each part of the funnel, for each product, and for each customer segment. This variety enables you to test various pieces of content with each outreach to see which garners the best response. Just because someone didn't respond to a demo doesn't mean they won't go for a free trial. They might respond better to a free quote offer than to a downloadable free tool or vice versa. Once you have the cohesive content stories in place, you can move on to designing the campaigns to deploy these pieces of content to prospects and customers.

Designing Campaigns

A demand generation campaign can take infinite forms. Most fall under one of three categories: lead generation campaigns, lead-nurturing campaigns, and upsell or cross-sell campaigns. To maximize revenue growth, you must master all three types of campaigns.

Campaigns to Generate Leads

In my experience, most companies struggle to build and implement lead generation campaigns that will help them acquire new customers. Usually, they're targeting potential customers that they haven't interacted with at all. That means their campaigns will need to focus primarily on the discovery phase to help customers understand their problems with more clarity and the consideration phase to showcase the benefits of their approach to solving the problem. They can do this in two ways: be visible where buyers hang out and make sure their public relations work contributes to their sales velocity.

Be Visible Where Buyers Hang Out

The absolute key to success in digital advertising lies in selecting the right online channels. If early in your business development you're not certain where your buyers hang out, the best place to start is Google. Everyone is on the internet, and everyone uses Google. Once you've mastered Google, you can move to other channels of advertising. To aid in your channel selection, ask your customers where they spend the most time online. What online communities do they hang out in? Which social media sites do they spend time on? What keywords do they search? Which online media outlets do they go to for information? Which bloggers do they follow?

Make sure to ask customers where they found you and what inspired them to go looking for you. These questions can reveal hidden gems. For example, if you offer firewall services and several of your customers say they found you because they got fed up with their old firewall provider," you'll know that a lot of your potential buyers will be searching for phrases like *[competitor's name] replacement*. So you can go out and buy Google PPC ads for relevant keywords.

Your competitors can also lead you to the best channels. Several online tools show how each channel performs for other companies. Once you know which marketing channels they're using, start with test campaigns to determine the level of engagement on each channel. Then show up in those channels. In my experience, the way to do this is through paid and unpaid advertisements.

In 2020, companies spent $1.4 billion on internet ad buys. Yet new research from the LinkedIn B2B Institute and System1 reveals that 75 percent of B2B brands fail to produce advertising that drives long-term growth. Obviously, many of these companies are having the same problem that John Wanamaker experienced over a hundred years ago, only worse! For this exact reason, I have never been a fan of paid advertising (Google PPC excepted).

If you do choose to go the paid advertising route, you must be laser-focused and intentional about your ad buys and personalize each ad to the customer you want to attract. Each platform provides different value, and some platforms that work well for one company do nothing for another. Choose the platforms best fit for your company. To do this, it's imperative to understand the value each channel offers. For example, search-advertising platforms such as Google AdWords work best when there is a clear demand for your product and you want to target people who search for your product online.

To effectively use this sort of ads platform, track the search terms that your customers are using, then buy space on the most important terms. Make sure your copy provides clear, immediate value, otherwise the prospect will move to another brand. Gevelber, recommends that you develop tangible ways to assist a customer in a micro-moment. For example, make the purchase easy with an Instant Buy button or develop comprehensive and free how-to videos that provide value.

If you work for a start-up with a new innovative product, then search engine advertising will not work as well. Nobody knows enough about the product to search for it. Instead, try social media advertising (Facebook or Instagram). Those platforms offer tools that allow you to buy highly personalized ads that show up on ideal buyers' feeds.

Finally, LinkedIn, with their user base of working professionals, is an excellent platform for B2B advertising. No platform allows you to target ads toward working professionals better than LinkedIn does. You can target users by job title, job function, and industry, so you can target your ideal buyer with unparalled precision. On top of that, you can include lead generation forms directly in your LinkedIn ads, which significantly increases velocity because prospects no longer have to navigate to your web page.

I much prefer unpaid campaigns to generate inquiries and leads. The main reason for this is obvious: they're free. Effective SEO is one great example of how to do this, but there are other creative ways to make sure you are visible where your buyers hang out without having to spend money on advertisements.

Once you have a list of the places where your buyers show up, work on finding ways to directly place content on those pages. Effective ways to do this is by building relationships with online publishers and bloggers, getting experts from your company to contribute articles to those publications, or guest blogging. You can also give interviews and seek other creative, mutually beneficial ways to partner with these channels.

For example, at Thycotic, we decided to launch a podcast called *401 Access Denied*. This podcast focused on breaking news in cybersecurity. But we knew it would take a significant amount of time and money to cultivate a large, regular audience. We also knew there was a successful podcast network at a company called Spiceworks that attracted a large listenership from our target audience. We approached them and offered to collaborate on a podcast on their network. We would provide a cybersecurity expert and creative twists that the audience would find interesting. They would provide the equipment, production, and the perfect audience. Spiceworks agreed, and *bam!* we had a successful, widely listened-to podcast with very little start-up costs. This brought loads of new visitors to our web pages, many of whom converted into leads and bought our products. The key to this type of strategy is to provide real value and not to make the podcast seem like an infomercial. We focused on issues and developments in the cybersecurity world. We occasionally mentioned our company, and we always linked to our website in the notes.

Launch a Community to Fuel Growth

In order to establish a community that contributes to revenue growth, you must provide the systems to facilitate conversation (e.g., forums, Slack, Twitch, etc.) and create regular programs that seed relevant content to spark new ideas among participants. According to my colleague Whitney Rothe, here is a simple road map to help you get started.

1. Define your community persona

Clearly define the target end user segments and the unique value proposition to establish your community persona. The persona should be consistent with the core value your product delivers and adjacent topics. To that end, we recommend that you start with the product use cases that have the highest adoption within your core group of customers. It will be much easier to build a vibrant community with the people who have the highest affinity for your products.

Additionally, you will want focus on end users first. Generally, you want people who are subject matter experts and are highly engaged in their field to contribute to the conversation.

Finally, you will want to evaluate where there are potential gaps in the knowledge base and broader market trends where your core end users will be qualified to and want to contribute. These topics must be product agnostic to attract observers who are interested in learning and engaging about the core subject matter but will not know your brand.

2. Establish your foundation

Once you have defined your community persona, it is critical to establish foundational community infrastructure, including documentation, forums, and technology to facilitate community interactions. As your community matures, you may need more sophisticated technology, but we recommend starting with a community platform. The community platform becomes the forum on your website where end users and your organization collaborate.

3. Recruit internal and external influencers

While you are getting your infrastructure in place, establish an inner circle of influencers who are both subject matter experts and well known within the broader ecosystem of your target persona. A deep bench of both internal and external influencers will attract new members, create content, and engage in conversation.

Start with your internal influencers: Identify both the key product experts and the personalities in the company who are most comfortable and capable of engaging with your community. In addition to assembling the internal squad, create a strategy to identify, prioritize, and recruit external thought leaders, based on their reputation, credibility, and the size and quality of their audience.

Building relationships with thought leaders with smaller reach, but who will regularly go to bat for the community, will help grow organic adoption, rather than recruiting rock stars in the space who are more superficially involved.

Both internal and external influencers should be leveraged as subject matter experts to establish the community as the destination for quality thought leadership. Establish SLAs for your internal team to post on the community forum and contribute to content at least 1–2x per month. You should be more strategic in how you engage external influencers but provide incentives to contribute to key community content.

4. Invest in programs to establish and activate your community

Once you have the foundational infrastructure and team in place, it is marketing's responsibility to run regular programs and seed relevant content to influence interactions and attract new members to engage with the community. Start by identifying the current community watering holes: external sites and meetups where target end users gather information and engage. This includes destinations such as subreddits, where users learn best practices from peers, and GitHub, where users collaborate on projects related to your solution. Finally, evaluate publications where end users go to learn about broader industry trends and from technical experts in their field.

Leverage Public Relations to Increase Sales Velocity

To fully maximize an HVDM strategy, make sure your public relations team directly contributes to lead generation. Unfortunately, all too often this isn't the case. In my experience, some PR teams want other people in the company to bring them customer success stories or game-changing ideas that they can pitch to media outlets. Instead, PR teams should focus on generating high-quality leads, boosting visibility, and giving current customers confidence in their buying decision. To do this, they must conduct primary market research, seek and sponsor awards, and execute rapid response PR.

Several PR teams already conduct and release primary research, but few do it effectively. Often, their research efforts focus narrowly on the products they're trying to promote. This compromises the credibility of the report, which erodes trust with potential buyers.

To be effective, conduct primary research on a topic that's top of mind for your customers. Present new insightful data that can help someone get smarter, see how their results compare to those of their peers, and improve their performance. The methodology of your primary research shouldn't be biased, and you must deliver real, reportable metrics that will inspire someone to handle a problem in a new way—and do it now. Once you've conducted this research and put it into a groundbreaking report, you can weave your marketing messages into the report by including your expert opinion.

For example, when I worked at PentaSafe, I quickly realized that if IT professionals could prove to their bosses why they need our software, our sales would skyrocket. So we developed a free online assessment that allowed people to see how vulnerable their systems were to being hacked.

After a while, we analyzed the responses of 1,350 individual employees from 583 companies and found that 23 percent of security officers consider their organization's security awareness as being dangerously inadequate, while an additional 44 percent consider their security awareness inadequate. Nearly six out of ten respondents receive a D or worse grade on security awareness and behavior. We published these results in what we called the *Security Awareness Index Report*, which we sold online for $195. Naturally, we gave it to prospective customers for free.

This report was groundbreaking, and we got a lot of buzz. But we pushed it even further and leveraged the results of our survey as much as possible. Based on the report's initial success, we started an independent Human Firewall Council that attracted notable members from businesses, governments, and universities. This council gave several keynote speeches at the biggest trade shows. At the same time, a small team at PentaSafe presented the results of the survey at regional events around the globe.

Did you notice the one thing I haven't mentioned? Our products. We never tried to peddle PentaSafe. That would have appeared too self-serving. Since we weren't hawking our products, we were able to get our annual report cosponsored by *Computerworld* magazine in North America, and *Computing* magazine in Europe. This led to even more awareness. And all that buzz and awareness attracted our target customers, IT professionals, to our website and the free online assessment. At the end of the survey, we always asked if respondents wanted to hear from our sponsors who offer solutions to their security challenges. Almost everyone said yes.

The beautiful thing was that we were the only sponsor, and we could pass everyone's information right along to our sales team as a qualified lead. Then the salesperson would follow up as an expert consultant. The first thing they would say was "how did you do on our online assessment?" More often than not, the answer was "bad." Together with the prospect, the salesperson would go over the results of the assessment. This allowed sales to zero in on exactly what the prospect needed and offer a tailored solution.

We constantly brainstormed new ideas, so we could regularly conduct assessments and build reports that would feed our PR and demand generation engines. I liked to implement two or three of these annually. This sort of PR-driven research can become a deep well for your business, providing a steady stream of leads, visibility, and content that you can repurpose for other campaigns. Write articles about the findings, lead webinars, speak at trade shows, and write white papers. The possibilities are endless.

When it came to seeking and sponsoring awards, I had a rule of thumb: if we could win a relevant award, I wanted it. I held my PR firm accountable for being on top of finding every one of them. Some people think that only a few of the big awards matter. Not me. I wanted to win a constant stream of them to build the impression that something spectacular was happening at Thycotic.

But winning awards is only half the battle. Another great way to create positive public relations while also generating leads and revenue is to give awards, especially when a part of the criteria for that award generates leads. You don't want that to be the full criteria—it will completely ruin the credibility of the award. But finding a clever way to use an award process to generate leads improves velocity. For example, at Thycotic we created the Partner of the Year award and invited all our channel partners to apply. Channel partners love stuff like this—when they win, it offers great visibility for their company and helps build credibility. Additionally, we offered a financial incentive by giving the winner a great margin on the sales they made.

When we announced the award, we sent out a press release and sent a message to all our partners, telling them that several of them were in the running, but we hadn't made our decision. We told them that verified deal registrations were one of the most important parts of our criteria. In an effort to win, they all focused on registering more verified deals. This is where the award really benefited us—each registered deal was a high-quality lead. In the run-up to the award announcement, we dramatically increased the number of leads that came from our channel partners, while improving our PR and that of our partners.

Used correctly, a PR firm can generate countless opportunities to improve visibility where buyers hang out, often at a low cost. At Thycotic, we achieved this by making sure our PR firm monitored every relevant publication, blog, event, and conference. Whenever an article or event came up that we could contribute to, the PR team alerted us, and we sent our domain expert to add his thoughts. Our expert gave concise, informative answers and drew from a deep well of knowledge. Speed here is key—writers typically have short deadlines, and "first to respond; first to get in" often applies. One last tip: Give your domain expert a big, sexy title. Titles matter. At Thycotic, we gave our expert the title of chief security scientist. This title was C-level, even though he wasn't on the management team, and we coined the term *security scientist* because it stood out, even though most people wouldn't know what it meant.

Additionally, if we were achieving success in important parts of the company, I made sure we publicized it. For example, we promoted the growth and success in our partner channel program, growth of our cloud products, and success in a vertical industry. I wanted to communicate good news and have our brand associated with success momentum.

Taken together, all the reports, speaking engagements, press releases, awards, blogs, and articles we landed fueled the perception that something special was going on at our company. Employees noticed and felt proud to work for a winner. Partners wanted to sign on with us. All the publicity drove traffic to our website and, more importantly, built trust with potential customers. Finally, competitors feared us and wasted time wondering why they didn't have the same momentum.

Lead-Nurturing Campaigns

Lead-nurturing campaigns have two primary functions: 1) to move an active prospect through the funnel and 2) to reactivate old leads. To do this, lead-nurturing campaigns need to keep your company front and center, answer questions from the prospect, and build trust with the prospect. They also need to further qualify a prospect by soliciting information. As with everything, these campaigns will differ from company to company, but effective lead nurturing has essential components: build nurturing campaigns for each audience segment and establish touchpoints and a cadence.

When you acquire a lead, you also receive a huge amount of information: the person's title, company, size of their company, and location. Based on the part of the website and content they interacted with, you also know what they're interested in. This knowledge is priceless—it can help you build campaigns that target very specific audience segments. Few tools perform better in advertising than highly personalized messages. Yet I still see several companies employ one-size-fits-all lead-nurturing campaigns, which almost always underperform.

I made a point to use the information we gathered to build the most personalized campaign possible. At Thycotic, we developed different lead-nurturing campaigns based on two main factors. The first was the prospect's title. For our privileged password management programs, we knew that in most companies, we had two kinds of potential buyers: the security executives (CISOs, VPs of security) and the IT operations people. These buyers had different must-solve problems and different concerns. The security executives focused mostly on making strategic decisions, keeping everything safe, and making sure they complied with internal policies and regulations. The IT Ops people were the product's end users, so they cared about ease of use and customizability. Once we captured a prospect's role, we would send them down different nurturing tracks, each designed to address their must-solve problems. The security executives received communications and content that focused on compliance and IT security, whereas the IT Ops people got content about how easy it was to use our technology and more information to help them gain a greater understanding of the vulnerabilities in their systems.

Second, we developed specific nurturing campaigns based on where the lead came from and what other content the lead interacted with. If we got the lead from a webinar, we would follow up with content directly linked to the topic of that webinar. If we got the lead from a free tool, we would put them in the free tool nurturing cadence. Finally, we built ready-made campaigns for our channel partners and allowed them to put their own names on the nurturing sequences. They could leverage our knowledge of the best way to sell our products, while allowing the channel partner to get the credit and build the relationship with the customer.

When building campaigns, decide which channels to use and how often you'll contact potential customers. The key is to strike a balance between communicating enough so you stay at the front of a customer's mind, but not so much as to be annoying. I suggest starting small with a campaign that sends out four or five emails over several weeks. Once you have that in place, start to experiment. Extend the time frame of your campaigns and add new touchpoints. Incorporate phone calls and other communication channels and vary the content and messaging. As your lead-nurturing campaigns become more sophisticated, make sure not to spam prospects. If you send someone a marketing email, a product launch announcement, *and* a newsletter in the same week, the potential buyer will probably unsubscribe. The best way to find out what works is to test and track open rates, leads received, number of unsubscribers, and the traction generated by various techniques.

Also, keep in mind that different lead-nurturing campaigns require different cadences. For example, if you're building a nurturing campaign for people who just attended a webinar, then it's most effective to send the first follow-up email within an hour after the end of the webinar. For a campaign designed to follow up after a trade show, then it's better to wait a few days to let the prospect get back to the office and settled in.

The High-Velocity Approach to Trade Shows

Even though digital demand generation campaigns comprised the core of our approach, we still invested in field marketing such as trade shows.

These events attract huge numbers of our ideal customers. Not many people attend a PAM trade show who aren't interested in PAM. Plus, if we didn't go, all our competitors would still be there. I had no interest in giving them a free foothold.

We took an aggressive, high-velocity approach to trade shows. This started with research. We made a list of all the upcoming shows and conventions and found out who planned to attend. How many of our current customers would be there? Would any companies we'd been targeting for a while attend? Our competitors? If we had attended in the past, what sort of return on investment did we receive? It costs a lot of money to send a team to these shows, and we wanted to maximize our return on investment whenever we could.

To reach that return, as I mentioned in chapter seven, we went into each show with a set of clear goals broken down into individual responsibilities. One of those goals was to have the most exciting booth at the show. To that end, our CEO once put his bright-green Jeep up for raffle. We literally hung the Jeep, a two-ton car, above our booth. Nobody could miss us. To enter the raffle, all anybody had to do was give us their information. In other words, become a lead. This created a frenzy. I'm sure that almost everybody there dropped by to see what was going on with a car hanging from the ceiling. Even if they didn't all convert to leads, they at least saw our name.

But, of course, the leads are the most important part. Revenue from a trade show almost never comes directly at the trade show but during the follow-up. That's where most companies go wrong. The first big mistake they make is to reach out to every lead right after the show. While this might seem like best practice, in reality it's when every other vendor sends their emails. Plus, it's when every buyer has just returned to the office and has to dig through a pile of work. Nobody has the time or energy to engage with a new brand. We always waited for at least a few days, and sometimes a week, before we reached out.

The other mistake people make is to dump all of the leads on the sales team. They think that anybody at a trade show would have at least some interest in the product, so they might as well have sales talk to them. The problem is that a lot of people don't want to buy at that exact moment. Sometimes they just come for the Jeep. To remedy that, the marketing team qualified all the leads first. This is where our trade show success relied the most on our HVDM foundation. We would put the leads into a trade show nurturing cadence and send them emails and content related to that experience. Some of the leads would interact with our content and accrue enough points to go to sales. Others went to the BDR team, and still others lapsed.

Upsell or Cross-Sell Campaigns

Existing customers are a gold mine that many companies do not fully tap. At this point, you already know a lot about the customer, their needs, budget, and industry. By building follow-up campaigns, you can leverage all that information to target the customer with emails, phone calls, and social media ads that offer the products that best complement their original purchase. For example, you might send a small business that bought the standard edition of your software an offer to upgrade to a more expensive version. You'd probably want to send information about adjacent products to a large company that bought the most expensive version.

A great tool for targeting existing customers is to offer webinars led by other customers. This builds trust and lets your customers compare their performance to that of their peers. A customer will be far more inclined to buy if they hear a peer talk about how they've successfully implemented your other products.

Measure and Optimize

Many companies struggle with measuring their demand generation performance, which means they're completely lost when it comes to optimizing and accelerating revenue. In my experience, this happens because they either focus on too few or the wrong metrics. They might keep track of the events they've been running, how many people attend their webinars, how many press releases they send out, and how many articles they placed. All of this completely fails to provide a clear picture of marketing's performance. Instead, focus on hard data. While the key performance indicators you choose to track might vary from campaign to campaign, there are several essential KPIs to track at each part of the buyer's journey, from discover through to purchase. Let's examine the KPIs for each part of the buyer's journey in more detail.

Discover

1. **Number of net new inquiries:** The net number of people who respond to digital marketing content for the first time. I like to divide these by source. Remember, the sales team needs qualified leads, not inquiries.

2. **Digital ad click-through rates:** Digital ad click-through rate is the number of clicks an ad receives divided by the number of times it is shown. This measures how well ads (and their placement) perform.

3. **Website traffic:** Website traffic is the number of new and total visitors. To make HVDM successful, try to make sure traffic increases every quarter.

4. **Website bounce rate:** Bounce rate tracks the percent of visitors who leave after viewing only one page. Visitors who bounce rarely become leads, so this number should be as low as possible.

5. **Website visitor duration and engagement:** Engagement measures how long visitors stay on a website and how many pages they visit. The more time, the better—it means the right people are finding the website, and the content engages them.

Consider

1. **Visitor-to-lead CVR:** Visitor-to-lead CVR indicates the proportion of website visitors who convert to leads. This metric is one of the strongest indicators of how well a website generates demand.

2. **Total leads by source:** The following are examples of lead sources:
   - Search
     - Organic
     - AdWords
   - Referral
     - Customer
     - Partner
     - Employee
   - Web referral (traffic sent from another website)
     - Referring website
   - Social
     - Twitter
     - LinkedIn
     - Facebook
   - Advertising (paid media)
     - Specific display ad campaigns

- Sponsored content (paid media)
  — Specific content download
  — Specific sponsored webinar
- Events
  — Specific events
- Business development
  — Tele-prospecting

Once you have all this data, you can identify exactly which channels produce the most and the highest-quality leads and invest more in the highest-producing channels.

3. **Lead-scoring distribution:** The lead-scoring distribution report is an important metric because it reflects the quality of leads, indicating how effective each of your marketing sources are and whether they're worth their cost.

Evaluate

1. **Lead to sales-accepted lead and opportunity CVR:** This is the percentage of leads that convert to sales-accepted leads as well as opportunities. It's one of the best ways to determine lead quality and whether the lead scoring is accurate.

2. **Total number and dollar value of opportunities:** This metric focuses on how many sales-qualified leads become an opportunity, or how many prospects are likely buy. Keep track of how much money you would make if you closed every opportunity.

3. **Pipeline coverage vs. revenue goal:** This measures the ratio of the dollar value of opportunities in the pipeline to an upcoming revenue target. It is a great way to see if you're on track to meet your goals. Since you will not close every opportunity, I've found that the only

way to consistently hit revenue targets is if your open pipeline is at least three or four times higher than the current goal.

4. **Lead-to-opportunity velocity:** The time (expressed in days) it takes a lead to convert to an opportunity.

Purchase

1. **Actual revenue vs. revenue goal:** This is the most important metric. It will show if your efforts have been successful.

2. **New customers added:** This shows whether you're increasing your customer base or relying on upsells and renewals to drive revenue.

3. **Opportunity-to-deal CVR:** This indicates the closing rate of the sales team. A low number could mean sales isn't doing enough to close deals, or it could indicate that marketing hasn't generated good enough leads. Or both.

4. **Opportunity-to-deal velocity:** The amount of time (expressed in days) it takes for an opportunity to convert into a deal.

5. **End-to-end CVR and velocity:** Often referred to as win rate, this is calculated by determining the total number of leads that convert into customers. Velocity measures the amount of time (expressed in days) it takes for a lead to convert into a deal.

6. **CAC:** CAC is calculated by dividing all the costs spent on acquiring customers (marketing and sales expenses) by the number of customers acquired in a given period. The lower the CAC, the higher the profit.

At every company I've worked for, we built a master dashboard that allowed me to track each of these metrics at a glance. These numbers will tell you how well a campaign performs and help you nail down the exact places, strategies, channels, and even content that drives the most revenue. Every day that I was a CMO, the first thing I did each morning was check the numbers. I made sure everyone on my team did the same, and they all started thinking in terms of improving these KPIs. It became such an ingrained habit for me that I still checked the Thycotic numbers each morning even after I moved out of the CMO role and into a chief of staff role.

The bottom line is that HVDM is a continuous cycle. Every time you build and implement something new, you get a new opportunity to deepen your knowledge and improve, to spark ideas, and even challenge your original strategy. Those realizations and challenges to your strategy can create fear and uncertainty at first, but try to embrace them. It's a good sign. It means you're open, testing, and poised to invent new, unique techniques to help you exceed your revenue goals every time.

CHAPTER 9

Get Results from Account-Based Marketing

O n almost any successful B2B website, the home page displays a series of customer logos. Airbnb. Microsoft. IBM. Big household-name companies. I call this a trophy collection. Everybody wants to win business from these giants. Yet to do so, you can't rely on HVDM alone. In larger organizations, the buying process takes longer, involves more decision makers, and requires more comprehensive research than in smaller organizations. HVDM alone rarely produces enough reach and momentum to convince all the decision makers in a large company all at once.

To win large clients, you need to become an expert in ABM. In the early 2020s, ABM was the hottest buzzword in marketing. All this chatter and excitement created a lot of unnecessary complexity and uncertainty. As with most buzzwords, everybody talked about it, but almost nobody could define it. As everybody rushed to implement it, a lot of people made mistakes, and marketing agencies started to aggressively push ABM on their clients. Many of these agencies convinced customers to launch expensive ABM campaigns that didn't produce anything close to the projected revenue.

In its simplest form, ABM is a strategy that targets multiple decision makers at large accounts. Instead of casting a wide net, organizations use ABM to blanket buyers at a single organization with highly personalized content and communications. The truth is that ABM, while a new acronym, isn't actually unique. It is simply a different way to apply some fundamental marketing approaches.

To me, it doesn't make sense to jump to an ABM strategy without a successful HVDM strategy. Early on in their development, a lot of companies estimate how much they would make if they landed a lucrative contract with a company like GM or Apple. Then they invest everything they can in chasing big fish. This rarely works, but it can serve as a launch pad for a company. More often than not, that strategy fails, and the company wastes huge amounts of money chasing accounts they will never win. The truth is that large companies rarely take a risk on a young company that hasn't proved that their products scale.

When I took over at Thycotic, it was a young company that had only closed one six-figure deal. We had employed a fast-follower approach, coming into the market with our PAM software after CyberArk. Many large companies had CyberArk. Initially, we barely sold to large companies. However, while CyberArk dominated the larger market, we didn't have much competition in the middle market. That's who we targeted, and I built up our digital marketing capacities to do so. Eventually, our digital ad buys and organic search content began to hit larger companies. We got a little action from them, leads, and even closed a few deals. At that point, I knew that we had a product that we could sell to enterprise.

On top of all of that, we had the resources to implement ABM. Part of that came from our HVDM foundation. We had a huge stash of content that could adapt to ABM purposes, and enough resources to maintain a sales team that could focus on large enterprises. When I saw this combination of sufficient resources and proof that we could compete upmarket, I invested in ABM. We generated sizable returns.

By the time I retired, we were winning several six-figure deals each quarter and had even started to close seven-figure deals on a regular basis. This chapter will show you the five keys to achieve similar results through ABM. Those keys are to construct the right ABM team, select the right accounts, target and tailor persona-based communications, maintain sales and marketing alignment, and measure and optimize.

Construct the Right ABM Team

A great ABM team starts with the sales and marketing leaders. They should oversee the entire process and assign the right (and often best) talent from their departments to ABM. Marketing provides the messaging, creates content, and executes the campaigns. The salespeople advise on account selection and follow up with those accounts. Try not to overload salespeople—they each will have to communicate with several buyers and influence each account. I never assigned more than three to five ABM accounts to a sales representative at a time.

Select the Right Accounts

When you target an account with ABM, you enter into fierce competition with a high cost of entry. Everybody wants these accounts, and most of them already have solutions that meet at least some of their needs. For that reason, pick your accounts carefully, or else you will invest a lot of time and money with little to show in return.

To ensure that we didn't waste money chasing unwinnable accounts, the VP of sales and I had to approve every ABM account. This mattered—we both had to agree, because both of us (and our teams) shared accountability for success. When we first started, we also made sure to limit the number of accounts we went after. It's easy to overstretch with ABM and invest a lot of money before seeing returns. We expanded to target more accounts after we were confident in our approach and success rate. While senior leaders had the final say, we incorporated input from several sources. First, we used our ABM software, which tracked online behavior and cookie data from corporate IP addresses (Martech, discussed in length in chapter five) to find large accounts in the market for a PAM solution.

Then we asked our sales reps for their input. They had to feel engaged and involved in the decision-making because ABM takes so much effort over a long period of time. If the sales rep doesn't feel excited about the account, then their follow-through tends to be sloppy, if it happens at all. More importantly, reps offer valuable insights about who is most likely to buy. Sales reps understand their region better than most. They will have relationships with business leaders in their region and will pick up on information about who is in-market. As much as ABM technologies help discover intent to buy, never discount the on-the-ground, firsthand experience of reps.

In all our decisions, we tried to play to our strengths. For example, Thycotic sold to a lot of midsize banks and financial institutions. Our sales team already knew how bankers think, feel, and talk, so we targeted them before striking into new fields. We also went after any accounts where we already had a foot in the door. Most often, that came in the form of one of our several partner organizations. Many of our partners had existing relationships with large companies, and we could work with them to cocreate unique packages tailored to those large organizations.

For instance, at Thycotic, we partnered with a Big Four consulting agency that worked with a large hospitality organization. That hospitality organization had suffered a data breach that became public news. I usually didn't make it a practice to chase down every large company that had been hacked. Hackings happened all the time, and whenever a large company was compromised, every single cybersecurity firm would call them the next day. I had no interest in profiting off somebody else's misfortune. Besides, because everybody in the industry targeted recently breached companies, it was one of the hardest times to actually stand out.

This time, we had an in. Our partner, the consulting firm, knew that the breached company wanted to change its cybersecurity provider. With our partner, we developed and executed an ABM strategy that targeted the hospitality company. Eventually, we sold it a package that paired our software with the consulting firm's assistance in implementing the products. Everybody won: Thycotic and our partner both secured large deals, and the buyer got a quick, easy-to-implement, and effective replacement for the failed system.

Aim to do something similar. Get creative, think about your partner organizations and how you can collaborate to accelerate ABM success. When you pair with a partner organization, you create a unique product that your competitors can never beat.

Target and Tailor
Persona-Based Communications

Everyone talks about one-to-one marketing, yet few actually do it. When is the last time you saw an ad that felt designed exactly for you? Has it ever happened? An ABM campaign offers perhaps the best opportunity to achieve one-to-one marketing because you know exactly which decision makers at which accounts will read each ad.

Before you design those ads, you need to know whom to target. Most large organizations make purchasing decisions by committee. At Thycotic, when we sold software to medium-sized companies, we only had to deal with the CISO, and maybe an IT operations leader. When we sold to larger organizations, we would have to target the CISO, several VPs or directors of IT, and compliance officers. Find out which titles at each organization have a say in buying decisions and who holds each position.

Once you've done that, craft tailor-made messages across the buyer journeys for each persona. Your main goal is to drive consensus for a purchase decision. That means that even while you target an individual, you do so in the context of their company. Work to connect the urgent needs of each decision maker back to the strategic objectives of their company. As with any other kind of content, avoid sales-y language. Try to educate and show how your product resolves their (and their company's) pains.

Research the company and its industry. What challenges is it facing? What are the new trends relevant to your product and solution? What do other people with the same titles that you're targeting say about the problem you will help solve? Knowing all of this will help you adapt the content you have (or help you make entirely new content) so that it drives ABM sales.

Draw as much as possible from your HVDM foundation. Start by adapting the value proposition to resonate with each specific buyer and use it to build content and messaging. For example, at Thycotic, a lot of our early enterprise wins came with large tech companies. We tweaked our value proposition to respond to why large tech companies required simplicity. Then we got more specific. We fed the CISOs and VPs of IT security content about how our simplicity made their companies safer because it reduced the risk of a human error breach. With the IT admin personnel, we focused on how the simplicity would make their jobs easier.

This level of personalization is the best way to compel buyers to act. Everyone skims on the internet, especially when reading any sort of ad content. People only stop to engage if they encounter something that resonates with them, that provides a *wow* moment.

Maintain Sales and Marketing Alignment

ABM relies on a steady stream of highly personalized contact between your sales and marketing teams and your prospect's key decision makers. To pull off such a complicated dance, sales and marketing must maintain alignment. And I mean total alignment. They must work in sync with one another and be in constant communication about who they will contact, how, and when. Marketing will usually deploy, in some cadence, a cocktail of emails (often containing content like assessments and white papers), PPC and retargeting ads, LinkedIn ads, direct mailers, and social media. Sales will follow up with phone calls, emails of their own, or messages on social media.

To execute their roles, both groups need to fully understand the accounts, the buyer personas' urgent pains, and how your solutions solve for those pains. Further, they must both have a clear sense of the specific content (white papers, for example) that marketing will deliver at each step so that sales can tailor their follow-up specifically to those materials. When I worked at Thycotic, I ensured this communication occurred by requiring our ABM teams to meet weekly, review lessons learned, and adjust accordingly.

For each buyer, I created an ABM multitouch implementation calendar (figure 4) to coordinate when and how sales and marketing teams would reach out. I included the calendar as part of an overall ABM playbook that outlined the full campaign from first contact through closing.

JANUARY						
SUNDAY	MONDAY	TUESDAY	WEDNESDAY	THURSDAY	FRIDAY	SATURDAY
			1	2	3	4
5	6 LinkedIn paid ads	7	8	9	10	11
12	13	14	15 Delivery of greeting card	16 Email LinkedIn InMail	17	18
19	20	21 Delivery of box	22 Phone call Email	23	24	25
26	27	28 Meeting Email	29 LinkedIn InMail Email	30 Phone call Email	31	

Figure 4: Sample ABM multitouch implementation calendar

Measure and Optimize

ABM sales usually take longer to close than sales generated through standard HVDM. This happens for several reasons. Larger companies make much larger investments, which means they tend to be more careful about where to put their money. They just tend to move slowly. They have more bureaucratic tape to cut, more complicated hierarchies, and more voices in the process. For that reason, an ABM strategy can usually take six months or more to bear significant pipeline and revenue. And that's why revenue alone won't tell the whole story of whether you're on track to achieve your goals. You might deploy effective ABM campaigns but not see any revenue for several quarters while the prospect goes through a lengthy review process. Likewise, a sales rep might develop strong relationships with key decision makers but not be able to report the account as an opportunity because they can't finish the BANT qualification.

Therefore, to measure and optimize ABM success, you need to track metrics other than revenue. An example of one of these metrics is account engagement. Figure 5 shows a sample report on this metric as well as if the targeted prospects converted into pipeline, revenue, or both. Notice the vertical axis tracks stages of engagement through to pipeline and revenue. On top is the total of both pipeline and revenue generated from the ABM campaign.

The most important metric to track, especially early on in an ABM strategy, is engagement. For each type of outreach you use, track how well it performs. How often do your targets open your emails and click on LinkedIn ads? If your mailers include calls to action, how often do those actions get completed?

Make sure to talk to the reps having the conversations to get qualitative data. Are they having success reaching the targeted buyers and setting up meetings? Does it seem like the targeted buyers are more excited about a certain piece of content than another? What companies that you've targeted are, in fact, in-market? If they are considering leaving a competitor, why do they want to leave that company? All of this can help you refine your messaging, both for ABM and for other HVDM techniques.

Once you get some momentum behind the ABM campaigns; you can start to track the amount of new pipeline and revenue generated. One benefit of the long sales cycle is that in some ways it can make revenue easy to project. You will gradually develop a sense of the sales cycle for the types of companies you're targeting and for the types of solutions that you sell. Then

	Pipeline $19,926,114			Revenue $3,215,970		
			ENGAGEMENT			
Account	Email Open	LinkedIn	Meeting	Opportunity	Pipeline	Revenue
Net New **September 20XX**						
Company A	•					
Company B		•	•			
Company C	•		•			
Company D	•					
Company E	•	•	•	•	$127,750	
Company F	•	•				
October 20XX						
Company A	•	•	•	•	$175,666	$175,666
Company B	•	•	•	•	$233,460	
Company C	•	•		•	$25,000	
Company D	•	•				
Company E	•	•				
Company F	•					
November 20XX						
Company A	•		•			
Company B	•	•				
Company C	•	•				
Company D	•					
Company E	•	•				

Figure 5: ABM sample report

you can project which open accounts will close in what quarter and for what amount. Once you have those projections, make sure to incorporate them into your revenue models (discussed in chapter seven).

The last metric to track is percent of accounts targeted vs. deals closed. Obviously, the higher you can get this metric, the better. It is difficult to accurately say what percentage of deals you should expect to close. There are just too many variables, including how many accounts you target, the need those companies have, and the sales cycle. All the same, you can work to optimize this metric by using the information you gain from the success of your campaigns to try to refine the accounts that you target in the first place.

Do you have the most success with ABM in a specific industry? It might mean that a lot of companies in that industry are realizing all at once that your competitor can't handle their needs. Are certain digital intent indicators converting at a higher rate than others? For example, does a flurry of searches from a company about your solution convert at a higher rate than companies that list available jobs for the people who will use your product, or vice versa?

The other way to improve this metric is to improve the campaigns themselves. This is where the engagement metrics come in. Don't be afraid to do some split testing with your ABM strategies, controlling as many variables as you can and mixing up the cadence and methods of communication. You might land on a formula that drives the most engagement and converts at a high rate.

CHAPTER 10

Create a Team of Marketing All-Stars

I believe Jack Welch, the former CEO of General Electric, had it right when he said, "Nothing matters more to winning than having A+ talent." I have seen small teams of A-plus performers run circles around much larger teams of B and C players.

This book covers a lot of ground, and it requires an aligned, high-performing team to successfully implement everything. To create a team of marketing all-stars, hire people with the essential qualities of A-plus performers, then supplement their efforts by hiring the right digital marketing agency and investing in marketing operations. Finally, you need to maximize that talent.

Hire People with the Five Essential Qualities of A-Plus Performers

I hear countless stories of companies with big problems that they can't solve no matter how much money they sink into them. They replace the person in charge of the problem area, and miraculously the problem disappears. People matter. In my experience, the right people aren't just the pure marketing experts, but also the ones who have the essential qualities of A-plus performers. You can always teach new technical skills, but you can't always teach these five qualities: the ability to set clear, inspiring goals; prioritize; embrace accountability; take calculated risks; and make tough decisions.

Essential Quality One: Set Clear, Inspiring Goals

HVDM is all about quickly hitting the right metrics. People who focus too much on vague goals like increasing visibility won't implement HVDM well. When I conducted interviews, I asked people to tell me about a big project they've led that moved the needle. I listened to how precisely they defined their goals, what levers they pulled, and how they inspired their coworkers to assist them. I was looking for people who wanted to make big impacts, compete, and win. I wasn't looking for people who compete for competition's sake or in a way that torpedoes a team. I wanted people who understood that the team's success was their success and that the competition was beyond the four walls of our company, never within. I sought out people who aimed to be the very best in their peer group. In short, I wanted people who understood that with the right efforts, we could become a leader in our field and outperform much larger teams.

Essential Quality Two: Prioritize

To achieve high velocity, a marketing team must focus on the actions and goals that move the needle the most. There's always another draft of content, more details to add to a projections model, and more ways to personalize a campaign. When employees don't prioritize well, it bogs down an entire operation and hurts revenue. For this reason, I hired people who knew how to read the metrics and trends and who focused on the actions that made the biggest difference.

Essential Quality Three: Embrace Accountability

There's a phrase that gets knocked around the start-up world: one throat to choke. Essentially, it means there should be one person held accountable for any given project. As a CMO, I made sure to surround myself with people who eagerly accepted responsibility for their projects. To produce extraordinary results with a small team requires dedicated work and seamless coordination. Neither of those are possible if even one person shirks responsibility and blames others when they fall short. Remember, if you're a leader of any kind, you need to set an example and always hold yourself accountable.

Essential Quality Four: Take Calculated Risks

When you think of Babe Ruth, what comes to mind? Home runs. In 1927, Babe Ruth hit his sixtieth home run of the season and set a record that would stand for thirty-four years. But the Bambino wasn't just the Sultan of Swat; he was also the King of Strikeouts. His risky all-or-nothing batting style sent him on a record number of triumphant trips around the bases as well as a record number of walks straight back to the dugout. The lesson: you won't hit a home run if you don't take a chance and swing. I'm not saying you should hire a bunch of sluggers who will swing out of their shoes at any opportunity. But you do need to find people who aren't afraid to take big swings at ripe pitches in game-changing moments. Those big swings can lead to tremendous results.

For example, while I worked for Postini, we wanted to find a way to boost visibility. After brainstorming for a while, we realized it would make a huge difference for us if we got coverage in the biggest newspapers and magazines. We made a list of all the biggest media outlets and worked to establish relationships with their writers and editors. At this time, spam was a recurring hot ticket news item, so a lot of them were glad to speak with us. At first, we just gave them quotes and statistics about spam for their articles. Eventually, though, someone on my team had an idea to create a map that showed where in the country the most spam messages came from. We told *USA Today* about this map, and they loved it. On a regular basis, pretty much whenever we updated our map, *USA Today* ran it on their front page. And right next to it was our name.

Our relationship with the *USA Today* writers deepened, and eventually one of them decided to do a long feature about cutting-edge anti-spam techniques. When they did, they talked to us. They asked us to recommend one of our customers they could interview for the article. That article was a boon for us—it mentioned our name all over the page. Between the coverage and our map, we saw exponential growth in our visibility. And we got more visits to our website, which led to more sales.

This wasn't the biggest risk—but it was a unique idea. It could have failed or led to less remarkable results. But my team and I embraced it, and we appreciated the chance to try something novel. It paid off in a major way. When I interview potential candidates, I look for people who light up when they talk about big out-of-the-box ideas that they'd love to try.

Essential Quality Five: Make Tough Decisions

A-plus players don't get stuck in analysis paralysis. I ask prospective team members to tell me about a big decision they made in their life and career, then assess how they made that decision. Did they solicit input from friends, family, and colleagues? Did they decide with a clear, high-priority goal in mind? How did they handle any fallout or unintended consequences?

Choose the Right Digital Marketing Agency

Few companies can afford a deep bench of people who are A-plus super-stars and HVDM experts. Chances are you will have to hire a marketing agency. Choose wisely. A bad digital marketing agency will ruin velocity, drain money, and damage your brand. It will focus on fluffy metrics and won't commit to helping achieve revenue goals. Then it will run campaigns that don't target the right people or focus on the right points.

On the other hand, an agency that understands HVDM can give a huge boost to the bottom line. It can even help bolster your internal talent. When I took over at Thycotic, it was all low-velocity marketing centered on in-person events and networking. We had some great people but not many who understood the digital world. I hired Integrous Marketing, my go-to agency. Whenever I hired them, I considered them a part of the team and incorporated them into our processes as fully as possible. This allowed us to hit the ground running—I didn't have to wait for everyone on my team to catch up and learn how to market digitally. And by working together with the agency experts and me, the team quickly became digital marketing experts. The woman who I replaced as the CMO stayed on the team. She was brilliant, creative, and hardworking. She just didn't understand digital marketing. After working with Integrous, she developed into a digital marketing leader I could trust to run everything with minimal oversight.

Sometimes it can be difficult to tell if an agency knows what it's doing. Most agencies sound great but ultimately fall short. After all, they are marketing agencies, so even the crummy ones know how to sell themselves. That's why I developed a scorecard that evaluates an agency's understanding of HVDM and whether it's likely to add significant value. I've divided the scorecard into six categories: digital demand generation expertise, knowledge of your company, campaign planning for all target audiences, campaign planning for all prospect touchpoints, provable contributions to revenue, and agency integrity. For each category, I provide questions to use to evaluate prospective agencies. While you can use this when seeking out an agency, be sure to go through the scorecard every few quarters. Doing this well help you judge whether the agency can scale with your business as it grows.

Digital Demand Generation Expertise

Digital demand generation is fundamentally different from branding, traditional advertising (TV, radio), or other engagement-based marketing. If an agency doesn't understand how to navigate the digital world, then they can't help you deliver the best possible results.

- Can the agency measure the performance of leads throughout the sales process?
  Yes = 1 No = 0
- Does the agency have certified experts in the marketing automation and CRM platforms your company uses?
  Yes = 1 No = 0
- Does the agency have a well-articulated process for projecting performance and making strategic adjustments to meet those projections?
  Yes = 1 No = 0
- Can the agency execute across all stages of demand generation? (Core capabilities should include digital media planning and management, creative development, landing page design and development, marketing automation, and analytics.)
  Yes = 1 No = 0

Demand Generation Expertise Subtotal: _____

Knowledge of Your Company

Many lead-based businesses sell technical products. Therefore, they rely on sales teams to close deals. Any agency that develops content for you must understand your business, products, and target audience.

- Does the agency truly understand your product or service?
  Yes = 1 No = 0
- Does the agency do a revenue breakdown of your business, including how much comes from new customers, existing customers, sales, and channel partners?
  Yes = 1 No = 0
- Can the agency track how many leads, opportunities, and wins come from paid and unpaid marketing sources?
  Yes = 1 No = 0
- Does the agency track the conversion rates of each type of lead?
  Yes = 1 No = 0

Business Knowledge Subtotal: _____

Campaign Planning for All Target Audiences

A comprehensive demand generation system should account for all target audiences.

- Does the agency have a clear breakdown of your ideal buyer personae, with campaigns designed to engage and convert each?
  Yes = 1 No = 0
- Does the agency develop campaigns to nurture active leads through the sales process?
  Yes = 1 No = 0

- Does the agency develop campaigns to reactivate dormant leads?
  Yes = 1 No = 0
- Does the agency develop campaigns that target your existing customers?
  Yes = 1 No = 0

Campaigns for All Audiences Subtotal: _____

Campaign Planning for All Prospect Touchpoints

A demand generation campaign must use all prospect touchpoints. These touchpoints include content that targets them, creative assets that engage them, web landing pages that convert them, thank-you pages and email programs that nurture them, and analytics systems that measure their behavior.

- Does your agency use highly targeted media and campaigns, such as ABM, to maximize return on investment?
  Yes = 1 No = 0
- Does the agency offer recommendations based on audience insights for generating creative assets that speak directly to buyers' pain points?
  Yes = 1 No = 0
- Does the agency develop highly personalized landing pages for each type of target buyer?
  Yes = 1 No = 0
- Does the agency create thoughtful thank-you pages and nurture campaigns that work hand in hand with sales messaging and processes?
  Yes = 1 No = 0

- Does the agency have a well-articulated plan for measuring and optimizing its performance at each audience touchpoint?
  Yes = 1 No = 0

All Touchpoints Planned Subtotal: _____

Provable Contributions to Revenue

While impressions, clicks, and leads are nice, none of them matter if they don't generate revenue. Any good agency will commit to growing revenue and then prove they have done so.

- Does the agency report and optimize based on opportunity and revenue performance instead of just on number of leads generated?
  Yes = 1 No = 0
- Does the agency track performance at the most minute levels, so it can not only choose the right tactics, but also optimize within tactics? For example, does the agency track performance of Google Ads down to the keyword level, so you can see which ad buys produce the most revenue?
  Yes = 1 No = 0
- Does the agency track exactly what marketing tactics reactivate dormant leads and opportunities
  Yes = 1 No = 0
- Does the agency set specific goals for its campaigns and hold itself accountable?
  Yes = 1 No = 0

- Does the agency provide always-on dashboards with up-to-date campaign performance?
  Yes = 1 No = 0

Provable Contributions Subtotal: _____

Agency Integrity

Trust is the foundation of any successful partnership. Marketing is an imperfect science, and every agency has imperfections, but working with a partner who you feel has your best interests at heart is critical for long-term success.

- Does or will the agency make recommendations that improve your marketing even if it might impact its bottom line, such as reallocating budget away from its activities?
  Yes = 1 No = 0
- Does or will the senior leadership work on your account day-to-day?
  Yes = 1 No = 0
- Do or will the agency tell you when a project is outside its expertise and help you source a vendor that can assist?
  Yes = 1 No = 0
- Does the agency charge an appropriate amount for the services it offers relative to its competitors?
  Yes = 1 No = 0

Agency Integrity Subtotal: _____

Grand Total out of 26: _____

How to Interpret Marketing Agency Scores

A perfect score is 26. Below is a frame of reference for how to evaluate agencies.

Scores of 22–26

If the agency scored a 22 or above, it is likely a great agency to partner with to pursue HVDM.

Scores of 16–21

If you're working with an agency that scored in this range, you may want to audit your demand generation programs and results to determine whether you're working with the right partner. Raise any issues you notice with your agency. If it can't address the concerns quickly, consider switching providers. If a prospective agency scores in this range, keep it as an option, but look for other agencies that score higher.

Scores of 15 and below

Scores in this range indicate several areas of significant concern. If you're working with an agency that ranks in this range, your results will probably be poor. If the agency hasn't proactively started to develop and deploy a solution to several of these concerns, I'd recommend finding a new partner. If a prospective agency scores in this range, move on and interview more candidates.

Invest in Marketing Operations

HVDM requires marketing teams to run like a well-oiled machine that incorporates internal stakeholders and external partners. But this machine quickly becomes complicated. To manage it well, you need to closely track scores of metrics while improving transparency, efficiency, and accountability. It is, in many ways, more difficult to manage marketing than ever. These new challenges have given rise to a critically important role: marketing operations.

A marketing operations leader or department acts as the marketing hub. They make sure that people, processes, technologies, and metrics all stay aligned. Essentially, marketing ops should do everything they can to make it so that the marketers themselves (CMO, content writers, webmasters) have as much time as possible to do their jobs without sacrificing key data or intelligence.

My marketing operations teams took responsibility for much of the nitty-gritty work that girds the processes described in this book. Team members managed and monitored our CRM software, collaborated with us on our lead-scoring models, and coded our software to reflect those models. They, likewise, took care of lead routing to make sure that we sent the leads to the proper salespeople or to the correct lead-nurturing campaign. They meticulously tracked where our lead opportunities and revenue came from (sales, marketing, channel), so we could easily create our revenue models. I also put them in charge of managing and maintaining our tech stack and training personnel to use it effectively. Finally, and most importantly, they managed the data. They cleaned it, stored it, processed it, and generated graphs and dashboards from it so our marketing leaders and I could quickly make the right decisions.

Get the Most Out of a Team

In my experience, when you have the right people, you need to let them do their thing. They're smart, creative, and driven. They likely know more than you about their jobs. I gave my employees the freedom to leverage their creativity and expertise to develop new ideas and initiatives. In short, they had the freedom they needed to succeed. Of course, I would provide direction and make sure that the marketing department stayed aligned. But I didn't micromanage, and if they performed, I didn't drop the hammer on any of them. I did, however, hold everyone to a high standard.

A-plus performers want to stay at the top of their field. They understand that they can't stay on top by doing what they've always done, so they take opportunities to improve. Don't make the mistake of letting them cruise. I pushed my A-plus performers to help them achieve their full potential. I made sure that I knew enough about every part of marketing to be dangerous to my employees, and then set up meetings to review what they were doing. We got into the details—not because I felt like I needed to control everything, but because the difference between good and great lies in the details. That, and because my employees almost always presented strong, polished, and well-reasoned plans. There was nothing to discuss but strategy and the details associated with successful execution. We reviewed metrics together. I asked questions and brought up perspectives they might not have considered. Then we edited and approved the plans together. Between their deep expertise, talent, and creativity, and my experience, perspective, and strategic vision, we created extraordinary results.

If they didn't perform, then I would quickly make the decision to move on. This wasn't to inspire fear or anything like that. Often, it is best to move quickly on decisions like these, both for the company's and the employee's sake. The employee can find a position where they thrive, and the company can find someone who fits their culture. When bad fits fester, they can infect an entire company. The other employees start to wonder why they are held to a high standard, while someone else gets to coast along.

In addition to what I've already described, I developed ten marketing commandments that I used to motivate my team.

The Ten Marketing Commandments

Just getting your team to buy into each of these commandments will go a long way toward maximizing their talent. But bear in mind that each commandment requires extra work. To abide by these commandments, employees will spend a little more time each day doing tasks such as researching, looking at metrics, and talking to customers. That extra work pays off—it makes their jobs easier and significantly improves their results. But not everyone can see those benefits immediately. So when I worked at Thycotic, I did everything I could to make sure the entire team adopted the commandments. I wouldn't just send this list out once and expect people to pick it up. I sent it out regularly. I followed up. I quizzed people, asking them questions on the spot about one of the commandments, not to make them feel uncomfortable or as a gotcha moment, but to make sure that they paid attention to what mattered. If you've managed to hire A-plus talent, they won't shy away from these questions. They will revel in them.

Commandment One: Know Thy Value (Proposition)

People buy differentiation. They will never pay a premium price for a product that is like everybody else's. A leader can do great work to come up with a flawless, compelling value proposition, but it won't matter if the team can't communicate it. I made sure that everyone who worked for me always knew and could communicate *exactly* why we were better than our competitors.

At Thycotic, we chose to focus on simplicity. We needed to establish at each part of the sales and marketing funnel that simplicity mattered in PAM software. This started with educational content about how important simplicity is and continued straight through to our free trials, which we designed to make sure that the parts of our software that showcased simplicity would shine through in our *wow* moments. That meant that the content writers had to understand our value proposition just as well as the developers building free trials, and the salespeople closing deals. We needed consistency in messaging, and we could only achieve that if everyone knew our unique value proposition.

Commandment Two: Know Thy Plan

Every marketer should know the marketing plan for each product, new and old, for at least two quarters ahead. This ensures that everyone executes according to plan. More importantly, however, looking this far forward reveals strategic opportunities that you might otherwise miss. For example, I consulted for a company that spent over a year developing a product that could help them break into new markets but only if they paired the launch with new positioning and messaging.

Unfortunately, nobody recognized the full potential of this product. Everyone, including the CMO, was too focused on the day-to-day operations to step back, survey the landscape, and think about the future. They did all the normal things they would do for a launch, but the opportunity to make a huge, attention-grabbing splash passed them by. Had they planned two full quarters in advance and shared that plan with relevant employees, they might have noticed the opportunity in time.

As CMO, I held regular meetings with my team, where we all stepped back from the grind and looked ahead. In our planning and discussions, we examined each product from every angle. Our best ideas came out, and we seized the biggest opportunities.

Commandment Three: Maintain Thy Sales Tools

Every quarter, marketers should produce or update five tools for each product they sell. Those five tools are a product brochure, a what's-new data sheet, a sales-training presentation, a customer-facing presentation, and a battle card. The product brochure is a customer-facing document that includes key features and pricing information about each product. The what's-new data sheet shows the product's new features, company changes, and shifts in the market. The sales-training presentation teaches salespeople best sales practices. Customer-facing presentations usually are PowerPoints designed to convince a prospect to buy. Finally, the battle card is an internal document that shows the most recent information about your company as well as your competitors and the best ways to battle and beat them.

A different team usually owns each tool, but they rely on the input from several stakeholders to finish the tool. For example, I would usually put product marketing in charge of the battle card. To create a thorough battle card, the product marketing people would need input from product managers, sales engineers, and salespeople who might have the most up-to-date intelligence about our competitors. At the start of each quarter, I wanted everyone to know exactly who they needed to contact to complete their tasks. This simple bit of planning prevents unnecessary delays and facilitates communication between functions.

Commandment Four: Know Thy Metrics

Everyone, not just senior leadership, should track revenue, pipeline, and expenses. Further, marketing staff should know how many customers they have for each product, especially for any product they have some direct responsibility for marketing, and how many customers they gain and lose. At the very least, I like to have people report on these numbers quarterly.

Commandment Five: Know Thy Customers

Everyone should talk to at least three to five customers per quarter. Not to merely solicit ideas for new features, but also to understand why they bought and what value they received. This reveals exactly what resonates with the target audience. Keep in mind that different functions will receive different customer feedback and in different ways. For example, product marketers might solicit customer success stories, whereas the webmaster might embed a feedback survey directly into the web page.

Commandment Six: Know Thy Competition

Competitors constantly make new moves. When they do, they usually don't send you a nice email to update you on their new tactics. They want you to ignore them, especially if they've found something that works or helps them poach your customers. As the leader, you should know all that you can about your top three competitors, what they have on you, and what you have on them. To that end, whenever my agencies or employees reported about our efforts, they also reported on our competitors' efforts. How had they changed their messaging and approach? How do they perform in terms of SEO rankings and PPC results? You can learn a lot about what resonates with the audience from what the other players do.

Everywhere I worked, I required my teams to track our top three competitors through the lens of their specific job. I wanted my webmaster to know about our competitors' website, my content writers to know about competitors' content, and my product marketers to know about competitors' products. We could find a lot of information online or by using tools that gave us access to some of our competitors' metrics. But we also relied a fair amount on our salespeople for our intel. We asked them what they had heard about our competitors and from our current clients, prospects, and other sources in their region. Because the salespeople knew that we cared, they took the initiative. Whenever they caught wind of some shift by our competition, they would report it to marketing. Then we would research the tip. If it was true and would help us improve our strategy, we thanked the salesperson in front of peers. This kept a steady stream of new information coming our way.

Commandment Seven: Know the Secrets of Thy Top Sales Reps

This commandment is not quite universal. I didn't care if my webmaster knew what made our top salespeople great. But I did need our product managers and content writers to understand this. While marketing trains salespeople on what to say and how to position the products, every great salesperson will tweak their message. Often, those tweaks make the difference between a great and an average rep. In their improvisations, they land on exactly what the customer needs to hear.

If marketing knows about these innovations, they can incorporate them into content development and overall product positioning. They can also use it to develop new training materials to bring less-than-stellar salespeople up to speed. Most salespeople focus on closing the next deal, which is good. They don't always realize that what works for them might help someone else. Extracting that knowledge and distributing it through the organization can make a sizable difference in revenue.

Commandment Eight: Know Thy Industry

To remain competitive, you must keep up on industry trends. There are several ways to do this. Analysts, such as the Gartner Group, regularly publish reports about various markets that can show trends in how customers spend money and think about their problems. These reports often reveal your market share at any given time. I recommend not only reading these reports, but also chatting with the analysts about their take on the industry.

Don't stop with the analysts. Read everything that comes out about your field or products. This will allow you to understand the top-of-mind issues of your target audience. For example, I set Google alerts for many topics related to cybersecurity, PAM, and passwords. As I was writing this book, I noticed a lot of new articles about a passwordless world. This was the hottest topic in cybersecurity, the idea that instead of relying on humans to remember passwords, we could use tools like two-factor authentication.

Because Thycotic dealt with passwords, a passwordless world would dramatically impact our business. I knew that it wouldn't be long before our customers asked us about a passwordless world, and I wanted to get ahead of the conversation. I did all the research I could. I wanted to know the feasibility, benefits, and risks of a passwordless world. My research revealed that the passwordless world could come to pass, so I thought about how Thycotic could adapt to providing security in such a world. Since this also impacted our salespeople and product development teams, I shared my findings with them.

Many of my best communication strategy decisions came from closely studying market trends. For example, earlier in my career, I worked for a cybersecurity company that assisted customers with regulatory compliance. At a financial analyst's conference, I happened to hear a leading CEO give a presentation on compliance. The way he framed the conversation around compliance seemed absolutely brilliant to me. I hadn't heard anything like it. That night, I went right to their company's website, hoping to read more about his perspective. But I couldn't find any of what that CEO spoke about. I was astonished. The talk had completely changed how I thought about compliance, but it seemed like the company didn't care about it.

Inspired by the CEO, I overhauled how we talked about compliance. I didn't copy what he said. It wouldn't have been applicable, as we both worked in different areas of cybersecurity. But I let his viewpoint influence how we thought about, and talked about, our company and its products. A few years later, that same company considered my company for an acquisition. That CEO and the rest of his executive team flew to where we were based. I gave a presentation to them about our company and how we positioned our products. I, of course, talked about compliance in the way that had been inspired by that CEO. When I finished my presentation, the CEO slapped the table, pointed at me, and told his team, "This is the kind of thing I've been saying for years!" Then they acquired us.

Great ideas can come from anywhere. It's natural to draw inspiration from other people who work in the same sphere. I'm not encouraging plagiarism. But keep an eye out for new approaches and new perspectives and consider how they might apply to your business. Check the influencers in your industry, the large companies with the best agencies and the biggest budgets, to see what they are saying. Then tweak messaging to make sure you can compete.

Commandment Nine: Respect Thy Colleagues

The best teams communicate. They lead with empathy; they listen to one another. They don't merely direct coworkers but come up with creative joint solutions instead. They respond to each other quickly. The absolute maximum amount of time to keep a colleague waiting for a response should be twenty-four hours. I usually respond in less than twenty-four hours. This is just a basic courtesy, a treat-people-as-you-want-to-be-treated rule. I consider this to be a universal rule, but it is especially important when communicating with salespeople. Usually, sales and marketing work in close concert, and salespeople rely on information from marketing to effectively do their jobs. When they reach out, make sure that whoever they contact on your marketing team gets back to them right away.

Being responsive matters. I've had incredibly smart, talented employees who just became black holes. I had to keep reminding them to respond faster—even to say that you're busy but will get back to them first thing in the morning. In the worst-case scenario, what starts out as a minor communication issue quickly spirals. It only takes one uncommunicative marketer (especially if they are a senior leader) to ruin the whole department's reputation. Suddenly, the sales team starts talking about how they can never get anything out of marketing. It torpedoes the relationship and impacts both departments' ability to do their jobs.

The best teams always say *please* and *thank you*. Not only does this help boost productivity, but it also makes your company a more pleasant place to work. Everyone knows what their coworkers are doing and feels respected and listened to at the same time. That sort of feeling is invaluable.

I modeled this behavior myself and expected the same from everyone who worked with me.

Commandment Ten: Celebrate and Support Thy Colleagues

During my career, I've been lucky enough to always work for companies that supported each employee and celebrated success. I'm always surprised by how many companies I've heard about that will post an amazing quarter without acknowledging the people who made it possible. Over time, that oversight alienates the highest performers. They start to feel like nobody notices their contributions, and they might jump ship. I made it a point to celebrate a strong performance and expected my team members to congratulate one another on any individual success. This reduced infighting and internal competition. People recognized that we won as a team and knew that everyone wanted the best for their colleagues.

A supportive culture also encourages employees to take more risks, which often pays off in big revenue-boosting ways. Nobody will pitch creative ideas in a culture of fear and rampant competition. I expected each employee to keep an open mind to new ideas and to support one another when someone took a risk. Then I modeled this myself. For example, at Thycotic, one of my employees came up with an idea to offer prospects a chance to win an all-expenses-paid trip to Naples, Florida, as part of an ABM effort. We got tons of interest but mostly for the trip—not for our product. In the end, we spent more on marketing and the Naples giveaway than we made back. Instead of blaming the employee who shared the idea, I took responsibility for it. I said, "Oh well. It didn't work." And we moved on. I made lighthearted jokes about the failed initiative in meetings, not to tell people it was okay that we lost money, but to show that it was okay to take a risk that didn't pay off.

When we were thinking of launching our podcast, this same employee had a brilliant idea to partner with an established podcasting platform that had all the technology and a wide following. We were able to launch our podcast to a huge audience at very little cost. Had I shamed her for the Florida failure, there's a chance she would have never shared this idea, which turned into a big win. She might not have stayed with us at all.

/////

In almost every company I've worked for, I had to go up against excellent, tough competitors. Even though I typically had a small fraction of their resources, my company almost always became an industry influencer. The larger companies would resort to copying us. At Thycotic, we focused on simplicity, and soon after, CyberArk made a similar pivot. We released a *PAM for Dummies* book, and CyberArk released a similar book months later. This only happened because of our stable of A-plus talent. People would get angry and tell me to go after these other companies for stealing what we had done. But we took it as a badge of honor—saw their imitation as flattery. And it didn't matter. Because while those companies rehashed what we'd already done, we plowed ahead, coming up with the next great idea that they would one day wish was theirs.

CHAPTER 11

Build Complete Sales and Marketing Interlock

Throughout my career as a CMO, I've seen plenty of companies where the sales and marketing teams battle one another. This always hurts the top and bottom line. Sales and marketing simply can't exist without the other. They must act as one to attract, engage, and convert prospects into customers in the shortest time possible.

As a marketing leader, I've made it a point to maintain a productive relationship with my sales counterpart because I recognize that sales and marketing have fundamentally the same goal: to increase revenue. Too many marketing professionals think their job is to increase visibility, generate content, or manage the website. They fail to realize that they must do all this in a way that contributes to revenue, and that is where most rifts open and velocity slows.

The first way to promote alignment is to make sure that everyone on the marketing team understands that the most important metric is revenue. I've made it a habit. I started each meeting with a recap of our target revenue for that quarter and what it was at the time. After a while, everyone else on the team picked up this habit, and soon each member of my team thought of their job performance in terms of revenue.

Beyond that, I have put in place a framework that leads to a sales and marketing marriage made in heaven. That framework has three keys: build goal transparency and synchronization, develop a stellar sales playbook, and stay connected.

Build Goal Transparency and Synchronization

Building goal transparency and synchronization sounds simple, doesn't it? Yet in many companies, the sales and marketing teams rarely meet to jointly set goals, assess performance, or coordinate actions. In my experience, these meetings should occur at least once a month. But the way you conduct these meetings also matters. Even when sales and marketing leaders convene, miscommunications arise, and teams miss their numbers. The key to maintain this transparency and synchronization is to agree on a single version of the truth.

Agree on a Single Version of the Truth

When you're tracking, analyzing, or reporting on status vs. goals, base your evaluations on numbers that each team agrees on. I've consulted for countless companies whose sales and marketing teams have different understandings of the goals and what each has to do to ensure goal attainment. When that happens, they waste tons of time just trying to figure out what is going on and how each team is performing. Then when something goes wrong, such as missing revenue targets, everyone defaults to needless finger-pointing. Nobody knows who was responsible for delivering what. Emotions take over. People fear that the poor performance will get them fired, reduce their raise, or hurt their chances of a promotion.

To avoid this, get crystal clear about quarterly goals and KPIs, including which teams own what KPI. In my experience, marketing should own these results:

- **Website visitor-to-lead conversion rates:** The percent of website visitors who become leads
- **Leads generated:** The number of new leads that marketing generated
- **Cost per lead:** Total marketing spending divided by number of new leads
- **Lead-to-opportunity and customer ratios:** The rate at which leads are being converted into opportunities and customers
- **Marketing-sourced pipeline:** The amount of pipeline marketing has sourced
- **Marketing-sourced revenue:** The amount of money marketing has sourced
- **Customer acquisition cost:** The amount of money it costs to acquire a new customer, which includes both marketing and sales spending
- **Marketing ROI:** The overall return on investment from marketing activities

On the other hand, sales should own these results:

- **Total revenue:** Total revenue (new, upsell, and cross-sell)
- **Sales- and channel-sourced pipeline:** The amount of pipeline sales or channel sources
- **Sales- and channel-sourced revenue:** The amount of revenue sales or channel sources
- **Sales growth:** The increase or decrease in revenue from two different time periods

- **Sales closing ratio:** The rate at which sales converts leads to customers
- **Average sales cycle:** The number of days it takes on average to convert a lead into a customer
- **Average revenue per account:** The average dollar amount per closed deal, which is often compared against CAC to determine whether the average customer can generate enough revenue to cover the cost of acquiring them

Both sales and marketing should own these results:

- **Customer lifetime value:** The potential value that a customer provides your business, which is often compared against CAC

Each team's responsibilities and day-to-day duties flow from the KPIs. For example, marketing needs to source a specific number of leads each quarter. Before the quarter starts, marketing can commit to delivering a certain number of leads to each salesperson. Then when a salesperson doesn't close enough deals, or if they complain about not getting enough leads, you'll know what went wrong to cause that breakdown. A quick look at the numbers will tell you if the salesperson did not get enough leads, or if they simply didn't convert the leads they received at a high enough rate.

If a sales rep did not receive enough leads, then marketing would need to get involved. I always left a little bit of my budget unspent for exactly these scenarios and used it to funnel leads to the rep. If the rep failed to convert their leads, then sales leadership would get involved and perhaps provide more training. This level of detail and alignment around goals will make it much easier for teams to proactively collaborate, while also enabling you to solve problems before they fester. With that clarity and alignment, you can then have far more productive and reasonable conversations.

During my career, whenever somebody blamed me or a member of my team for a failure, I wouldn't engage with them based on opinions. I demanded that these conversations rely on numbers and facts. If marketing agreed to source a certain amount of pipeline for sales, and then sales missed their revenue numbers, sales might blame marketing for sending them crummy leads. But we would have to look at the actual numbers. Did marketing source the right amount of pipeline based on its goals? Were lead-to-opportunity conversion rates in line with the goals? What about opportunity-to-revenue conversion rates? Because we all knew what we were supposed to deliver, we could see who was accountable and what went wrong, and know how to fix it. If I made the mistake, I would own up and do everything I could to remedy the problem.

As part of the responsibilities, make sure that you establish service-level agreements with the sales team about lead follow-up. When you've done everything right, elapsed time is the single biggest killer of deals. The longer a sales cycle stretches, the greater the chance that something beyond your control will halt the deal. The budget might disappear, the decision maker you targeted might get promoted, fired, or switch jobs. The company's priorities might change. This is why velocity matters, and this is why salespeople should follow up with leads quickly. A service-level agreement holds the sales team accountable for following up with leads in a specific time frame. The actual agreements vary, usually depending on how hot the lead is. At Thycotic, we prioritized the hottest leads, and we expected sales to follow up with those leads within twenty-four hours. Find whatever works best for your company—what matters is that you align with sales and do everything you can to quickly convert leads to customers.

Finally, your CRM must be the system that gives you a single version of the truth. When you're tracking, analyzing, or reporting on status vs. goals, you must do it from one system that everyone uses. Unfortunately, I've seen teams with personnel who didn't use their CRM system properly. It leads to a huge amount of wasted time, dysfunction, miscommunication, and, most importantly, missed opportunity.

Develop a Stellar Sales Playbook

In sports, a playbook contains the strategies to ensure that your team achieves the ultimate objective: winning. In sales, as in sports, you must coordinate actions to win. Therefore, you need a sales playbook to keep the entire team aligned and moving in the same direction. Essentially, the sales playbook contains all the most important pieces of information that will help sales reps close deals.

This resource makes training sales personnel much easier. Before a new rep starts, they can read the playbook and come in with foundational knowledge. Requiring new sales reps to do this before they start selling helps produce better results faster. But it also helps support existing reps. Every company wants all salespeople to perform as well as their top sellers. While that is difficult to achieve, an excellent sales playbook will help salespeople get as close as possible.

A rep can't expect to become a master after reading the playbook once. They also need to be trained. At the companies I've worked for, we used the playbook as the sales bible and organized our training around what it covered. I knew that people under stress often default to their old, unproductive habits. Therefore, we drilled the playbook until everyone internalized it. To make sure they understood and could use the concepts, we regularly tested employees.

To make the best sales playbook, assemble a team of subject matter experts. I invited the VP of sales, product managers, and technical sales support personnel (those who demo technical products) as well as our top sales representatives from different geographies to join the team. Together, we compiled all the pertinent internal documents and details. I always specifically asked the top sales personnel to bring the best materials they regularly used. We audited almost all of our existing collateral, call scripts, battle cards, training materials, web content, and analyst reports.

Nothing in business remains static, and the playbook is no exception. Whenever you add a new product, decide to change part of your messaging, or experience a shift in market position, update the playbook. And the playbook doesn't have to remain internal. I shared a version with our channel partners and let them adapt it to fit their specific needs as they sold our products.

The Thirteen Chapters in a Great Sales Playbook

While the pertinent information for a playbook depends on the company and industry, every playbook I built had the same basic type of information in it. I divided those into thirteen chapters. I'll go into detail about what to include in each chapter. After that, I'll provide a one-page template that you can use for quick reference to all the chapters as you construct your own sales playbook.

Chapter One: About Your Company

If someone were to say to a sales rep, "Tell me about your company," the rep should start with this chapter. I opened this section with a general introduction, including what we did, our size, and our market share. Next came our history. I added statistics about our history and performance, and wrote about our most impressive customers and how we helped them achieve great results. I listed each key industry or product award we had won, and, most importantly, laid out our company's overarching value proposition.

Chapter Two: Business Development Strategy

This chapter describes what is expected from each role on the sales team. Ideally, an employee should read this chapter and understand their top responsibilities and how leadership will evaluate their performance. Start by defining each role—for example, the differences between an account manager, a channel manager, and a business development representative. Then lay out the top responsibilities and KPIs for each role.

In this section, define each stage in your sales process according to your CRM best practices. For example, define the differences between an inquiry, a lead, a sales-accepted lead, and an opportunity. Include an in-depth breakdown of your BANT qualification procedure, including how to report opportunities as pipelines (covered at length in chapter six). This keeps everybody who's using the CRM software on the same page.

Next, describe what sales personnel must do when they receive a lead. Simply define each step of the process and give concise guidance on how to best execute each one. At Thycotic, our sales process followed these steps: discovery call, demo, trial and proof of concept, proposal, and then (we hoped), close. You will go into much more detail about each of these later in the playbook, but at this point, your goal is to give an idea of the entire process at a glance.

Chapter Three: Your Ideal Customer Profile

Define your ideal customer profiles in as much detail as possible, such as size of company, titles and top responsibilities of buyers, and influencers involved in the purchasing process. Go deeper to include the pain points of each buyer and the questions sales reps should ask to expose the pains. For example, at Thycotic we targeted systems administrators. Our playbook explained key responsibilities of system admins, their top pains, the questions to ask to expose those pains, and how our product could serve as a solution.

Chapter Four: Crafting Your Message

The goal of this chapter is to help sales reps diagnose where a prospect is in their buying journey and know what to say to move them to the next stage. As such, it also defines the buyer's journey. This is always one of the longer chapters because it goes into granular detail about the sales process for each buyer persona and each product or group of products. To keep salespeople from getting lost in the details, you need a guiding light. Start with a concise, powerful elevator pitch.

The best salespeople ask the best questions. Smart questions help them understand the prospect's problem and exactly how they would benefit from the salesperson's products. For that reason, before going into detail about how to craft messages for each product, compile a list of excellent questions. For example, some of our go-to questions at Thycotic were if the prospect knew how many privileged accounts they have and where they are located, and if they have all of their privileged accounts locked in a password vault. Usually, the answer to both would be no. We had other questions, but often these two were enough to get the prospect to realize they needed help. From there, it was up to the salesperson to ask follow-up questions that revealed the exact nature and extent of the prospect's challenges.

The rest of this chapter gets into the nitty-gritty of selling—the best practices of how to communicate the value each product offers, such as the key features and benefits. These should be short and sweet, just the best kernels of information, so a salesperson can quickly reference it while they're on a sales call. To back up those bullet points, include additional information such as case studies, analyst reports, and customer sound bites. All the things that build credibility with a customer should be right at the salesperson's fingertips, so they can pull from it whenever needed.

Chapter Five: Effectively Executing the Sales Process

This chapter is relatively simple. It provides an overview of how sales reps are expected to sell. For example, how many calls are each salesperson expected to make per week and quarter, and how many demos should they schedule to have a fighting chance of reaching their quota. The point is to communicate the company's expectations. At Thycotic, we would get into more detail about each procedure in chapters six through nine.

Chapter Six: Introductory Call

This chapter covers how to best make an introductory call with a lead. At Thycotic, we told reps how to conduct their pre-call research by reading about what the prospect does, what their needs are, and by examining any recent behavior that might indicate an intent to buy. We reminded the reps to focus on qualifying the company, not just the specific person who filled out the online form. The person who filled out the form might not have the power to make a purchasing decision, but that wouldn't always disqualify the company. That person might have been doing research on behalf of the actual buying decision maker, or they could have diagnosed a problem in their company and would be happy to refer the rep to the decision maker. Then we provided best practice scripts for calls and sample emails. Since this section focuses on prospecting, we only gave guidance on making initial contact. If the salesperson got in touch with the prospect, then they would look at later chapters about how to qualify and ultimately close deals. If they struggled to make contact, we provided scripts for further attempts to get an initial conversation. The scripts revealed how to cut through the noise and break through to prospects based on a deep understanding of their specific needs.

Chapter Seven: Qualifying Opportunities

This chapter describes best practices for BANT qualification. It includes sample questions about budget, need, and timeline, among other concerns. It also describes how to ask if the prospect was considering other solutions, and, if so, which other solutions. This is important because it helps reveal who you are competing against. That way, your sales reps could draw clear distinctions between us and the specific competition.

Finally, this chapter offers open-ended questions to help the sales reps quickly understand if the pains discussed are actual priorities. For example, reps can ask where does this problem rank on a scale of 1 to 10? Why is it so important? What would happen if you do not address the issue? Also included are questions to help move the prospect to the next step in the sales process, such as when can we set up a time to talk more about your specific requirements? Would you be interested in getting a personalized demo of our product? Would you like to try our product for free? And, if so, what would be the primary goals we need to achieve during that trial?

Chapter Eight: Discovery Call and Demo

This chapter covers how to execute an effective product demo for a customer. At Thycotic, we split the demo process into two steps: a discovery call, which came after the prospecting or opportunity-qualifying call and the demo itself. We wanted our salespeople to use the discovery call to get more information about the prospect, the company the prospect worked for, and their exact PAM needs. The earlier qualifying calls mostly dealt with the same topics but on a broader level. In the discovery call, we wanted to know exactly what technical capabilities the prospect needed to see in the demo and what would wow them. Then we wanted our sales reps to check in about the aspects of BANT qualification to make sure there hadn't been any changes to such details as the budget, timeline, or purchasing power that might impact the sale.

One key tip for discovery calls is to always ask at the beginning what the prospect hopes to get out of the demo. A lot of organizations don't realize that different customers have different needs, and the best demos address those specific needs. If a salesperson knows what the prospect cares the most about, they can tailor the demo to get right to the most important elements, instead of just showing off everything they can do. The playbook also reminds salespeople to check in with the prospect regularly. Thycotic salespeople would ask questions like, "Does this make sense?" "Does this respond to your specific concerns?" "Are there other capabilities that you want to see?" Most demos only run about thirty-minutes, and salespeople need to maximize that short window the best they can.

Our salespeople would then use what they had learned from the discovery call to design the demo they would present to the prospect. They would also pull the pieces of supporting content such as white papers, analyst reports, free tools, and product fact sheets that they thought would best support the demo. As with everything else, the more personalized a demo could be, the better. My playbook outlined how to give the demo, starting with introductions, asking the prospect again what they hoped to achieve, and continuing with how to slow down the demo to draw attention to the aspects of the product that would most appeal to the customer. Then based on how the demo went and how enthusiastic the prospect seemed, we provided guidance on how to either close the deal or move to a proof-of-concept trial.

Chapter Nine: Proof of Concept and Proposal

If a prospect doesn't buy after a demo, then the salesperson can offer a free trial. This chapter covers the best practices of how to successfully set up that free trial and then make a final proposal to win the business. At Thycotic, we made sure our salespeople understood what, exactly, the customer needed to see from a trial and how that prospect intended to evaluate the trial. Before a trial started, the salespeople would follow up with the trial objectives and success criteria written out in a one-pager. This is a vital part of the process—it allows the salesperson to remove any sort of ambiguity and gain consensus of how you and the prospect will judge success.

The proposal part of this chapter is far more cookie-cutter. Almost all of our proposals at Thycotic followed a similar template, so I just included examples of proposals for each product and each size of business that we served.

Chapter Ten: Objection Handling and Competitors

In this chapter, I collected the most common objections or concerns that my salespeople had to contend with and worked with the top sales reps and product managers to write copy that guided our reps' responses. The highest-performing representatives know better than anyone else what to say to move the needle. I trusted them to provide the expertise, and so should you.

I included battle cards showing the difference between our products and the products of our key competitors. There is an art to this conversation, however. You don't want to prime sales reps to bash competitors. Remind them to bring everything back to the facts. They use battle cards to draw clean, provable lines between your company and the competition.

Chapter Eleven: CRM Usage

This chapter helps clarify your expectations for proper CRM usage. The playbook is not a replacement for CRM training. It augments that training by providing a simple cheat sheet that covers the most important tasks every sales rep must complete, and it serves as a reference if they forget some of their training.

Chapter Twelve: Pricing and Negotiation

In the B2B sphere, buyers are literally professional buyers. Many receive training in how to negotiate. Just about every potential buyer will balk at the sticker price and ask for a discount. If your salespeople don't know how to handle these requests, they will get killed in every deal. This chapter covers exactly how to negotiate. My philosophy around negotiation is simple: use the buyer's requests as an opportunity to accelerate the sale. At Thycotic, we told every salesperson never to offer a discount without a concession from the customer. Ideally, we wanted the customer to commit to finalizing the deal by a certain day or become a reference.

To win that concession, we trained our salespeople to speak to the person with the ultimate buying authority as soon as possible. Some companies have a multilevel negotiation process, where salespeople must talk to two or three people before they reach the true financial buyer. At each level, the prospect asks for a steeper discount. We had no interest in watching our margin disappear like that, so we instructed sales to negotiate only with the people who had the final say. Sales then offered the discount, but on the condition that the deal would close by the day the customer agreed to. We essentially created a deadline for the deal and an expiration date for the discount. This also gave us an opening for check-in calls to remind the customer to act before their rate disappeared. I didn't mind giving a small discount if it meant we closed more deals quickly.

Chapter Thirteen: Resources

In this chapter, I included full descriptions and links to the most important resources a salesperson might need to close a deal. For example, free tools, analyst reports, and company- and product-specific presentations.

The links in this chapter led to a single up-to-date online repository that contained all sales and marketing materials that we produced. I also maintained a marketing calendar (in the repository) that showed when we would kick off new marketing campaigns and initiatives. Whenever we generated new content, we notified everyone on both teams, so everyone could review and use the materials.

Whenever you launch a new campaign, you should take it a step further and train the sales team before it goes public. That way, when they contact leads, they understand the marketing materials and the best way to follow up. If this sounds basic, that's because it is. A staggering percentage of success doesn't stem from brilliant new ideas, but rather from rigorous execution and discipline. To this day, I can't believe how often marketing teams launch campaigns without a single salesperson knowing a thing about it.

Sales Playbook: Sample Template

Chapter One: About Your Company
- General introduction
- Company history
- Company key talking points (reach and results)
- Solution overview

Chapter Two: Business Development Strategy
- Sales roles and key responsibilities
- Sales process
- Sales and lead stages

Chapter Three: Your Ideal Customer Profile
- Customer profile and persona—(defined in-depth)
- Customer pains and challenges
- How the company's products solve pains and benefits received

Chapter Four: Crafting Your Message
- Questions to ask to expose pains
- Layered elevator pitch
- How to communicate product value—key features and benefits and the typical *wow* moments buyers have
- Case studies, analysts' quotes, and other third-party validation

Chapter Five: Effectively Executing the Sales Process
- Outbound prospecting and other expectations around sales activity

Chapter Six: Introductory Call
- Objectives and outcomes of an introductory call
- Pre-call planning
- Outbound prospecting process
- Sample voice mails, scripts, and emails

Chapter Seven: Qualifying Opportunities

- BANT qualification explained
- Qualifying questions and how to determine actual priorities
- When and how to include an opportunity on a forecast

Chapter Eight: Discovery Call and Demo

- Sample discovery calls: what to say, show, and send
- Demo meeting best practices
- Post demo follow-up

Chapter Nine: Proof of Concept and Proposal

- Outcomes and objectives
- Roles and responsibilities
- What to say, show, and send

Chapter Ten: Objection Handling and Competitors

- Common objections and how to handle them
- How to beat top competitors

Chapter Eleven: CRM Usage

- CRM cheat sheet

Chapter Twelve: Pricing and Negotiation

- Pricing overview and links to related resources
- Sales negotiation best practices

Chapter Thirteen: Resources

- Description of materials and sales tools with inserted links to the sales resource center

Stay Connected

Ideally, everyone on the sales and marketing teams understands the entire sales and marketing process. I made sure that new hires in both departments attended the same onboarding program. That way, each new hire can understand and appreciate what their counterpart does.

Sales and marketing should also attend the same continuing training, with very few exceptions. Often, organizations train sales teams on how to talk to customers, how to beat competitors, and what the next versions of products include. But they neglect to invite marketers who work to position the products on behalf of sales.

Sales and marketing should also stay in close communication during day-to-day operations, especially at the leadership level. For example, in a sales leadership meeting, marketing can present what's on tap each week or solicit input on a specific topic. In a marketing leadership meeting, sales can give feedback on what's working or what needs to be improved. If your company has functional quarterly business reviews, each group should attend. I invited either a sales leader or a rock star salesperson to many of my marketing meetings and asked them to give a presentation about their experience on the ground. I included sales leadership in quarterly and annual planning to ensure we stayed aligned.

Remember that marketers, more than many other professional, risk locking themselves in an ivory tower. Unlike salespeople, marketers often don't have to talk to customers (or prospective customers) to fulfill their day-to-day duties even though they absolutely should. Yet of any group within a company, marketers should understand the customer the best. This is because marketing brings the company's strategic vision to life. For example, at Thycotic, we focused our company positioning on simplicity because we knew customers valued easy-to-use products.

We knew this because we got out of the ivory tower and learned about how complexity negatively impacted their jobs. Once we made that positioning decision, we worked with departmental leaders to ensure company-wide alignment with that positioning. R&D developed simple, easy-to-use products. Our sales reps emphasized simplicity in their conversations. We incorporated simplicity into everything we did, including contracts, customer support, and professional services. We did all of this because we knew what customers wanted and because each of these details set us apart from competitors.

The best marketers do everything they can to stay out of the ivory tower. I've already spoken about how I created a customer advisory board and encouraged my team to do the same. I likewise created a sales advisory board, which included the best sales reps and channel partners. I would reach out to them regularly and ask what they learned from prospects, how the prospects responded to our marketing, and what pieces of content they found to be the most effective and why.

On the flip side, I'd ask about the deals they lost and if we could make changes in our marketing to reduce the chances of future losses. You can learn just as much from knowing what stops people from buying your products or choosing a competitor, and that's something that the sales reps know best.

The sales team can provide marketing with a fresh, vital perspective. Marketing can do the same for sales. The two departments need to stay as close as possible to learn from, lean on, collaborate with, and support one another. Every company will, inevitably, face the challenges of flatlining revenue, a dip, or even just a moment when it seems like a quarter might go off the rails and spiral out of control. In those moments, interdepartmental rivalries can flare up. But those are the moments when the connection needs to be the strongest, when both teams together develop the solutions to challenges together. One cannot exist without the other. And when they work in concert, they can achieve extraordinary things.

EPILOGUE

This book covers a lot of ground. If you came out of it feeling overwhelmed or unsure of where to start, I understand. Channel that flare of anxiety into excitement. Transforming marketing from a low- to high-velocity approach takes time, effort, discipline, and coordination. But it offers incredible rewards.

At every company I've worked for, I inherited a team of digital marketing novices. In our initial meeting, I painted a picture of the incredible success we would achieve through HVDM. I told them about how leads, opportunities, revenue, and market share would explode. I promised them that they would become the best marketing team in the industry. That their business card would impress their peers, that people at trade shows would stop them to marvel at how impressive our work was. And I assured them that this success would cause our customers to love us and our competitors to fear us.

Were they a little skeptical? Of course. But I saw the excitement in their faces. They knew, innately, we could win big together. As we started to grow fast and achieve our goals, that excitement grew.

I could make these promises because I knew that if we implemented the methods in this book, we would achieve breakthrough revenue growth. I could tell that my team was hardworking, eager to learn new skills, and really wanted to make a positive difference. They just needed to learn a new, more effective marketing approach. I've always considered myself an in-the-trenches CMO. I could develop a strategy, of course, but what I really loved was to work arm-in-arm with my team, to throw myself into our processes, our campaigns, the metrics, and everything else. I knew that if we all worked together with commitment and dedication, we would achieve levels of success never before viewed as possible.

Share this book with your team and other key stakeholders in your organization. Then come together and discuss each chapter. Align and stay focused on the main goal—growing revenue. Start with an honest assessment of your performance, and look for quick wins. Write down the one or two immediate actions that will make a difference. Then go out and do them. This will give you momentum. You will feel the energy build and the excitement with it. If you feel the need, have a kickoff event. Share the vision with everyone around you. Invite them on this journey. Acknowledge that there will be trials and errors and learning and late nights. But ask them to go on the beautiful ride with you. It will be fun, you will achieve remarkable results, and you'll have done it all together.

ACKNOWLEDGMENTS

Over the past thirty plus years of my career, I've been fortunate to have collected so many meaningful and memorable experiences. Now I feel especially fortunate to write a book that draws from those experiences and shares them in valuable ways. This process has led me to reflect on the meaningful people and relationships that have made it all possible.

My list begins with my loves. My wife, Terry, my love always and forever, who has been by my side through every step of this incredible life journey. For more than thirty years of marriage, she has made our house a loving home and has sacrificed in many ways for me, our family, and my career. She is the CEO of our home, and I am forever thankful for her love and for her passion for motherhood as we raised our two wonderful children.

My children, Christopher and Jennifer, have become such successful, accomplished young adults who I am immensely proud of. My third child is my son-in-law, Ryder. We couldn't have chosen a more perfect son-in-law if we had tried. My fourth child is my daughter-in-law, Jackie, who we are happy to welcome into our family.

My grandchildren, Hunter and Savannah, who are my number one play partners. I love watching their smiles and laughter light up a room. They put life and work in perspective.

Acknowledgments

My mother, Laurie Stone, who is an inspiration to everyone. She recently beat breast cancer and is the best mother in the world. She has taught me so much about what true accomplishment really means.

My father, Harvey Kahan, who inspired us to outwork everyone, and that value has served me well.

My siblings Dave Kahan, Larry Kahan, and Andrea Biwer, and their children Lexi, Rachael, Beth, Brandon, Sarah, Chase, Lea, and Scott, who collectively create our large, loving, close-knit, and supportive family.

My list continues on the professional front, and I am grateful to each of the following people.

Special thanks to those that directly contributed great content to this book and made it much better. These four people are at the top of their profession and provided expert contributions to help make this book possible:

Carolyn Outwaite of EngineHounds is the best SEO expert I've ever worked with by far. If you want to improve your Google rankings, hire her. Carolyn can be reached at caro@enginehounds.com.

Josh Frankel of LogicBoost Labs is an incredible webmaster. He worked for me for many years, and his websites performed at incredibly high levels, which helped us grow revenue every quarter.

Marjorie Agin of Centerboard Marketing is one of the best brand experts and content writers I know. She has an incredible ability to grasp virtually any product and help a company connect with buyers and get results. Margie can be reached at margie@centerboard-marketing.com.

Josiah Sternfeld is president and CEO at Integrous Marketing. His company is the absolute best HVDM agency on the planet. Josiah can be reached at www.integrousmarketing.com.

I truly appreciate that Mike Triplett, Jonathan Cogley, Hugh Burnham, Darren Guccione, Francine Geist, and Phil Vorobeychik believed in me by investing in this new book to help businesses leaders around the globe achieve better business results.

Acknowledgments

My book team, who helped me turn my ideas, even the ones I thought were gibberish, into this cohesive work that I can be proud of, feel good about sharing, and that I hope will inspire readers to discover their own greatness that exists inside. These professionals include Robin Colucci, Dylan Hoffman, and my literary agent, Linda Konner. I also want to thank Matt Holt and the wonderful team at BenBella Books for helping me bring the book to market.

My colleagues who provided great inspiration and guidance to help me succeed at levels I never could have imagined. I'm forever grateful to these stellar individuals that include Simon Azzopardi, Doug Erwin, Kevin Klausmeyer, Jim Legg, John Ortbal, Chris Smith, Damon Tompkins, and all the start-up leaders, marketing team members, coworkers, mentors, competitors, investors, vendors, and consultants who have helped shape my career and whose examples have inspired me in so many ways.

I'd like to thank the scores of men and women who have called me friend at the many stops along my journey, and who have honored me with their easy laughter and hard truths. My life is richer for knowing each of these individuals who remind me daily how truly wealthy I am.

INDEX

Page numbers followed by *f* and *t* refer to figures and tables, respectively.

ABOUT THE AUTHOR

Photo by Jenise Millsaps

Steven Mark Kahan has successfully helped grow seven start-up companies from early stage development to going public or being sold, resulting in more than $4.5 billion in shareholder value.

Bringing passion and positive energy, Steve inspires teams and their organizations to take on the impossible and succeed. He is best known for his ability to plan and execute marketing strategy so companies can accelerate revenue, grow market share, and consistently deliver superior returns for shareholders.

In his previous position as Thycotic's chief of staff, he helped take the company from $10 million to over $110 million in five years. The company was acquired for $1.4 billion in 2021. It's been a similar story with the other companies, including KnowledgeWare, eSecurity, PentaSafe, Postini, BindView, Quest Software, and the Planet, where he's brought his talents over the past three decades.

In a rare move, Gartner Group recognized Thycotic in its 2018 PAM Magic Quadrant as having superior marketing in its peer group. And *Web*

Host Industry Review recognized Steve as Marketer of the Year in 2009. Steve was also nominated for the 2019 Cybersecurity Marketer of the Year. He has been featured as the ideal CMO by a Summative.com white paper, which used Steve as a model to help its clients hire the best CMO for its start-ups.

Steve's first book, *Be a Startup Superstar*, is the perfect complement to this book because it teaches readers how to ignite their careers in a tech start-up even if they know virtually nothing about technology. Connect with Steve at www.stevenmarkkahan.com.